CW00950452

AMAZING AND EXTRAORDINARY FACTS

CHURCHILL

CHURCHILL

Joseph Piercy

RP
RYDON
PUBLISHING

A Rydon Publishing Book
35 The Quadrant
Hassocks
West Sussex
BN6 8BP
www.rydonpublishing.co.uk
www.rydonpublishing.com

First published by Rydon Publishing in 2016

A CIP catalogue record for this book is available from the British Library.

ISBN: 978-1-910821-07-7

Printed in Poland by BZ Graf S.A.

CONTENTS

INTRODUCTION

In a 2002 poll conducted by the BBC for a series of programmes entitled *Great Britons: The Great Debate*, a late surge of votes for Sir Winston Churchill denied his nearest challenger, Isambard Kingdom Brunel, of the accolade of being voted as the greatest

Briton ever. It is arguable which of the two achieved the greatest lasting legacy, yet in the hearts and minds of the British people Churchill remains a titanic figure, often evoked and mentioned in times of trouble.

So what is this peculiar fascination with Churchill that holds such sway over 20th-century British history? There are detractors, of course. The Marxist essayist and critic Christopher Hitchens long railed against what he perceived, with some justification, as 'the cult of Churchill'. Critics cite the refusal to analyse his record as a politician both before and after World War II. Other

Churchill as a new Member of Parliament in 1901

charges against Churchill include: the stubborn and irascible nature of the leader's personality, the hubris, the petulance, and the overly artful, and to some eyes and ears wilfully pretentious, nature of his speeches.

The extraordinary aspect of Churchill's life is that it is hard to think of any major British event or issue that took place in the first half of the 20th century with which he wasn't either directly or indirectly involved. From the last knockings of the Second Boer War and developments in the welfare state, through World War I, the General Strike, Home Rule in India, and the abdication of King Edward VIII, and on to his greatest triumph as Prime Minister during World War II, Churchill was there.

The word 'genius' is easily and rather lazily applied; likewise, the term 'polymath'. Yet although my personal politics are, quite frankly, in opposition to those of Churchill, other than perhaps during his early years as a Liberal Member of Parliament, I'm prepared to stick my neck out on this and declare that Churchill was a polymath – as a brilliant writer, dedicated historian, dazzling orator, talented landscape painter, fearless soldier, and as a skilled and intuitive military strategist.

I have always felt that the term of genius can only be bestowed upon people who are flawed in some way; figures whose verve and drive has perhaps, at times, pushed them into dark water. History is a narrative and there would be no stories if the great, monumental characters didn't have to struggle or fight to have their voices heard and their visions and actions fulfilled.

Churchill certainly had a few 'blips' during his long career, so I feel it is important to acknowledge these. I don't believe it lessens his reputation – on the contrary, I feel it enhances the measure of the man. Churchill found himself 'on the ropes' several times – and arguably on the floor a few times in the knock-about boxing ring of politics and public life. Most importantly however, he managed to get up again before the count of ten and live to fight on. Quite how he survived the debacle of British intervention at Gallipoli, or other controversies such as his ill-fated tenure as Chancellor of the Exchequer in the lead up to the Great Depression, is a lesson itself in fortitude and resilience in the face of potentially personal and professional catastrophe.

Often overlooked, the role of Churchill's wife, Clementine, is also worth mentioning. He had, by all accounts, an unruly temper, especially when feeling pressurized and stressed. In a letter to her husband in the early days of World War II, shortly after Churchill had taken over as British Prime Minister and de-facto Commander-in-Chief, Clementine warned Churchill that his overbearing manner, irascibility and rudeness risked alienating his staff and damaging his effectiveness as leader.

I have tried, as far as possible, to put aside my own political allegiances and to be as even handed as I can when compiling this book of facts about, in all truth, an amazing and extraordinary figure of British history. The history of World War II alone could fill a whole library full of books. In a meeting with Franklin D. Roosevelt and Jospeh Stalin in 1943, Churchill is alleged to have assured his two Allied leaders that 'History will judge us kindly'; when Roosevelt supposedly questioned why Churchill was so sure of his statement, he is said to have replied 'Because I intend to write it'. Although any book on Churchill cannot possibly avoid his role as Prime Minister during what he himself proclaimed as 'Britain's darkest hour', it is a daunting task for any writer to pit themselves against a Nobel Prize for Literature laureate. For this reason I have chosen not to skirt over Churchill during World War II, instead trying to unearth some of the facts that are, for whatever reason, little known or often passed over.

Churchill in 1940

I'm unsure quite how I personally feel about

Churchill after researching and compiling this book. My own grandfather, Franco-Antonio Wiltshire, served in the Royal Air Force as a radio operator and rear-gunner for Bomber Command during World War II – this was an experience that, like many of his generation, he rarely spoke about in the post-war years, apart from the odd glib remark or dark joke. When he died in 2002, it became apparent to the rest of his family that he had been awarded several service medals for the number of missions he was involved in. But he had never bothered to claim them, and had refused to turn up, for reasons unknown, to ceremonies after the war. In another curious discovery, my grandfather never again set foot on an aircraft once the war was over.

I don't know what my grandfather would have said about me writing a book on Churchill. I think he liked the man, or at the very least admired him – and I'd like to think that he, like Churchill, did what was necessary at the time. I'd like to conclude these prefatory notes with a tribute to both my grandfather and Winston Churchill by quoting an excerpt from the latter's famous speech, delivered to the House of Commons on Wednesday 20 August 1940 at the height of the Battle of Britain, where he highlights the key role played in the war by British airmen:

The gratitude of every home in our Island, in our Empire, and indeed throughout the world, except in the abodes of the guilty, goes out to the British airmen who, undaunted by odds, unwearied in their constant challenge and mortal danger, are turning the tide of world war by their prowess and by their devotion. Never in the field of human conflict was so much owed by so many to so few. All hearts go out to the fighter pilots, whose brilliant actions we see with our own eyes day after day, but we must never forget that all the time, night after night, month after month, our bomber squadrons travel far into Germany, find their targets in the darkness by the highest navigational skill, aim their attacks, often under the heaviest fire, often with serious loss, with deliberate, careful discrimination, and inflict shattering blows upon the whole of the technical and war-making structure of the Nazi power.

Joseph Piercy
Brighton, 2016

Churchill in 1943

Unhappy childhood
*Parents conspicuous in
their absence*

Sir Winston Leonard Spencer-Churchill was born on 30
November 1874 in a bedroom
within the regal residence of
Blenheim Palace at Woodstock,
Oxfordshire. Although this would
seem to be a fitting entry into the
world, given that Blenheim Palace
was the private home of the Dukes
of Marlborough, Winston arrived
two months prematurely. It is
therefore safe to say that his place of
birth, despite his ancestry, was more
by accident than by design.

Winston Churchill's father was
Lord Randolph Henry Spencer-
Churchill (1849–95), the third son
of John Spencer-Churchill, 7th
Duke of Marlborough. Meanwhile
Winston's mother was Jeanette,
Lady Randolph Churchill (née
Jennie Jerome; 1854–1921), an
American socialite and the daughter
of the US millionaire stockbroker,
Leonard Jerome. Lord Randolph
was a prominent politician of the
day, with something of a reputation

Randolph Henry Spencer-Churchill

as a magnificent orator and a
tenacious opponent – traits
emulated by his eldest son Winston
in later life. In fact, Randolph was
a rising star in the politics of the
late Victorian era, going on to
hold the post of Chancellor of the
Exchequer under the Conservative
Prime Minister, Lord Salisbury.
However Randolph's outspoken
views, and his attempts to reform
the Conservative Party from within

to make it more progressive, led him to become increasingly sidelined.

Meanwhile Winston spent his early years living in Dublin, where Randolph served as an unofficial private secretary to his father, the 7th Duke of Marlborough, who Prime Minister Gladstone had appointed Viceroy of Ireland. A combination of his father's position and growing interest in politics, and his mother's busy social life, meant that Winston had very little contact with either of his parents during this time. Yet he was overseen by a governess and his nanny, Elizabeth Ann Everest. Mrs Everest, or 'Woom' as she was known (see 'Woom'), was the closest person to Winston during his childhood.

When the Churchill family returned to London for Randolph to further his political ambitions, Winston was sent to boarding school in Ascot, which put further distance between himself and his parents. Although always respectful of them in his memoirs, many historians have speculated on the effect that the subsequent long periods of separation had upon

the boy. His relationship with his father is particularly interesting, as Winston seemed to crave Randolph's approval – but rarely seemed to receive it. Although Winston thrived at his second preparatory school in Hove, Sussex, it appears that neither of his parents made much effort to visit him there (see Fresh Air). Similarly, the prestigious 'Speech Day' at Harrow School was often attended by Winston's nanny, Mrs Everest, while his parents remained conspicuous in their absence.

When Winston, at his third attempt, gained entrance to the Royal Military College at Sandhurst, Randolph is thought to have been disappointed that his son chose to train as a cavalry officer rather than with the infantry. Winston's choice is thought to have been made on the grounds that it was easier to obtain a place at Sandhurst with the cavalry, as it was a process that didn't require any aptitude with mathematics. Although Winston flourished at Sandhurst and graduated with respectable grades, Randolph was again dismayed when his son didn't subsequently transfer to the infantry, as he was entitled to do.

Lord Randolph Churchill died in 1895 aged just 45, only two months after Winston graduated from Sandhurst. Many of Randolph's biographers have speculated over the cause of his death at this early age. It was thought by some that he might have contracted syphilis, although when or how this could have occurred has long been purely a matter of speculation and rumour. However, developments in medical science suggest that Randolph's illness and death were more consistent with an undiagnosed degenerative brain disease. At the same time, some Churchill biographers, such as Sebastian Haffner, have suggested that his father's death spurred Winston on to make his mark upon the world as quickly as possible, believing that he, like his father, would die young. In the event, Winston Churchill was to live twice as long as his father.

'WOOM'

Mrs Elizabeth Ann Everest (1832–95) was Winston Churchill's nanny throughout his formative years (see Unhappy Childhood), and his closest friend and confidant. Churchill referred to her as 'Woom' in his letters and correspondence – this may stem from his early attempts to speak as an infant and gain her attention, 'Woom' being a rough approximation of 'woman'.

Mrs Everest – the 'Mrs' is thought to be an affectation, as she is not believed to have ever married and died a spinster – joined the Churchill household in 1875 soon after Winston's birth, initially as a service maid and housekeeper. But with Lady Churchill showing little desire for the trappings of motherhood, Mrs Everest was soon elevated to the position of nanny. Churchill wrote to his nanny frequently while he was away at boarding school, and she replied with affectionate and encouraging correspondences.

When Churchill entered Sandhurst, it was decided that Mrs Everest was surplus to requirements – somewhat unceremoniously, she was dismissed from her post. Churchill is thought to have been appalled by his parents' harsh treatment of his beloved nanny after her many years of loyal service, and he wrote to his mother to protest. Elizabeth Ann Everest died two years later in 1895 of peritonitis – Churchill covered the arrangements for her funeral and paid for a headstone. According to Churchill's son, Randolph, his father also paid an annual fee to cover the upkeep of her grave for several years following her death.

Fresh air
Attending preparatory school in Brighton

Churchill had a chequered academic career, which began when he entered formal schooling at the age of eight. Initially Churchill attended St George's Boarding School in Ascot, an experience that he describes in his memoir *My Early Life* (1930) as 'horrible'. A frail and often sickly child, with a mop of red hair and afflicted with a lisp and stammer, the young Churchill became a prime target for bullying. Mindful of the effect that such unpleasant experiences were having upon their son's development, Lord and Lady Randolph Churchill subsequently moved their son to a small preparatory school in Hove, near Brighton in Sussex.

This school was run by two sinister sisters, Charlotte and Catherine (Kate) Thomson, who taught lessons alongside a staff that consisted of two female governesses, one male Classics tutor, three female servants, and a matron. When Churchill arrived at the school in 1884 aged ten the school consisted of 16 boys, many of whom had been born in British colonies in India and Africa.

The rationale for sending Churchill to a relatively obscure preparatory school in Sussex appears to have hinged upon his weak constitution. Brighton had a reputation as a health spa in Victorian times, so it was thought that the fresh sea air and the close proximity of the Churchill family doctor, Robson Roose, would ease concerns about Churchill's health. However, the fabled south coast sea air did not have quite the desired effect upon Churchill's fragile health – he became severely ill with pneumonia on one occasion and nearly died.

The Thomson sisters ran a rather unconventional school, where their pupils were encouraged to identify areas of study that interested and engaged them. Churchill developed a love of literature, particularly poetry and history, and he excelled in physical pastimes that included swimming and horse riding. His frequent letters home to his parents and devoted nanny, Mrs Everest, suggest that he enjoyed his time in Hove, although he complained about the standard of the school meals.

By his own admission Churchill was 'a troublesome child', and despite settling at the school the adolescent Churchill experienced his fair share of skirmishes with authority. A letter from Charlotte Thomson dated 17 December 1884 recounted an incident in which Churchill was stabbed in the chest after quarrelling with another student during an art lesson. Churchill's injury was minor – but according to Ms Thomson, he had instigated the fight. In a separate incident, Churchill was disciplined for refusing to adhere to conventions during the mass that the school's pupils attended on Sundays at the Chapel Royal in Brighton. Churchill is thought to have refused to turn to the east during the reading of the creeds, out of respect for his staunchly Protestant nanny, Mrs Everest.

In March 1888, Churchill

travelled to Harrow, the prestigious public school, to attend an interview and entrance examination. Charlotte Thomson accompanied Churchill on the trip, later recounting how the boy was so nervous that he vomited outside the exam room. Churchill's strongest subjects were history, literature and geography, but the entrance tests for Harrow also required him to demonstrate his aptitude in classical subjects such as Latin and Greek. Churchill did just enough to scrape a pass, entering Harrow School the following month.

*Blue plaque to commemorate
Churchill's schooling*

HISTORICAL ERROR

*The Thomson's preparatory school
(see Fresh Air) was relocated to
premises in the nearby Sussex
town of Haywards Heath in 1898.
Nevertheless, the people of Hove
commemorated Churchill's place
of schooling by unveiling a stone
plaque on the site of the original
school at 29–30 Brunswick Road
in 1953.*

*Unfortunately, the dates of
Churchill's time at the school were*
*incorrect on the original plaque: it
cited the years 1883–85, as opposed
to the correct dates of 1884–88.
And even when the stone plaque
was replaced by a heritage blue one
in the 1980s, the dates were still
not corrected.*

*Today Hove Council periodically
receives angry letters from
Churchill scholars and historians,
demanding that the error be
rectified. However, as the plaque
was funded by private donations,
removing and replacing it is beyond
the council's jurisdiction.*

Distinctive diction
Turning a potential problem to an advantage

Winston Churchill has always been easily identifiable by his distinctive diction; however, this was a cause of great concern for him when initially considering a career in politics. He always had a problem pronouncing his 's's correctly – an impairment he appears to have inherited from his father, Randolph – and feared this would cause problems when it came to public speaking in the political arena.

Therefore, in 1897 he visited the renowned speech therapist, Sir Felix Semon, to seek help in overcoming his impediment. Semon reached the conclusion that there was nothing physically wrong with Churchill and that, through practice and perseverance, he could learn to master the impairment. Interestingly, and rather intuitively, after his first consultation with Churchill, Sir Felix is reported to have remarked: 'I have just seen the most extraordinary young man I have ever met'.

Felix Semon

In his usual dogged manner Churchill did persevere, practising such phrases as 'The Spanish ships I cannot see for they are not in sight' and other similar exercises, which, he was advised, would help to cure his problem. In any case, he was certainly not deterred from public speaking, and after one exceptionally well-received oration he is said to have declared 'My impediment is no hindrance'.

Later, when constructing his many famous speeches, Churchill deliberately avoided as many words as possible that began and ended with an 's'. When he did use such words, they appear to have had no adverse effect – rather, they seem to have added to his charm. One of his well-remembered mispronunciations was 'Narzees' instead of Nazis.

For many years, experts have disagreed on whether Winston Churchill's speech impediment was a stammer or a lisp. During the 1920s, and again in the 1940s, writers mentioned that he suffered from a stammer – but the general consensus today seems to be that he in fact suffered from a lateral lisp. Specialists now know far more about stammering, which is thought to be a specific neurological impairment in the brain. This is a condition most typically exhibited in children aged between two

and five (especially in boys), the majority of whom eventually completely recover.

Descriptions of the young Churchill by his family and close acquaintances make no mention of him having a stammer. And later, none of the many secretaries who worked for Churchill ever referred to his hesitation while dictating – any pausing was thought to be due to him searching for the appropriate words. Characteristically, Churchill turned a potential problem to his advantage – he was a politician whose voice was, and still is, instantly recognizable. In addition, many actors have played Churchill on both the stage and screen (see Lights, Camera, Action!), and the unique quality of Churchill's voice no doubt presented a considerable challenge for them to sound authentic.

American Churchill
Discovering a literary namesake

In the late 1890s Churchill was embarking upon a fledgling career as a writer and journalist, primarily as a means of supplementing his income as an officer in the British Army. Lady Randolph Churchill had used her contacts in the London media to first secure for her son the role of war correspondent for *The Daily Graphic* during the Cuban War of Independence (1895–98). Then, when Churchill was posted with his regiment first to India and then to the Sudan, he continued to send back reports from the front line that were published in *The Pioneer* and *The Daily Telegraph* – these reports and recollections were subsequently collected in his first published work, *The Story of the Malakand Field Force* (1898).

It was during this time that Churchill discovered he had a famous namesake, also a writer. As Churchill was preparing for the publication of his second volume of reports on the Madhist War in the Sudan, his attention was drawn to notices in the British press that advertised a forthcoming publication: a novel entitled *Richard Carvel* by an American author named – Winston Churchill.

Concerned that their respective literary careers could become confused in the eyes of the book-buying public, Churchill wrote to his American counterpart. His letter proposed that in future all of *his* published works would bear

The American Winston Churchill

the signature of William Spencer-Churchill (his full name), leaving the American Churchill free to use *his* own name. Churchill also suggested that the future works of both writers should include a short note to differentiate between the two authors. He concluded his letter by complimenting the American Churchill on his success as an author, although there is little evidence that he had actually read any of his works at that point.

The American Churchill replied to the British Churchill that he was in full agreement with the proposal, proffering his apologies and explaining that he would have changed his penname had he known, but that he was christened without a middle name. In the event, Churchill didn't go on to use his full name on his future works, crediting them instead to William S. Churchill.

During a trip to the USA the two Churchills met one another. Striking up a mutual friendship, they continued to correspond with each other right up until the American Churchill's death in 1947.

SAME NAME, DIFFERENT STYLE

Winston Churchill (1871–1947) was a prominent and popular American novelist in the late 1890s and the early decades of the 20th century (see American Churchill). The American and his British counterpart not only shared a name and an occupation as authors, but also enjoyed many of the same interests. Both men were keen and accomplished landscape painters, although the British Churchill favoured oils over the American's penchant for watercolours. In addition, both men were interested in history and politics, although again the American Churchill wrote mostly fiction, whereas the British Churchill wrote only one novel, Savrola (1900).

The American Churchill had a brief dalliance with politics and sat on the state legislature for New Hampshire in the first decade of the 20th century, but he retired from politics after failing to become elected as Governor for his adopted state in 1912. At the time that

Herbert Asquith

Churchill encouraged his new American friend to enter into politics. It is suggested that he had a plan to one day become Prime Minister of the UK, while his counterpart would be President of the USA – thus the free world would be governed by Winston Churchills.

Great escape
Flight from a POW camp

the American Churchill was retiring from public life, the British Churchill was playing a prominent role as a member of Prime Minister Herbert Asquith's Cabinet. The American Churchill retired from writing novels in 1917, publishing just one final book in later life – however he was unable to replicate the success of his earlier career. Meanwhile the British Churchill continued writing and publishing well into his 80s.

There is an apocryphal story: when the two Churchill's met for the first time, Winston Spencer-

By 1899 Churchill had become a seasoned war correspondent, having covered campaigns in Cuba, India and the Sudan (see American Churchill). Yet the event that brought him firmly into the public consciousness was his daring escape from a prisoner-of-war camp in Pretoria during the Second Boer War (1899–1902).

In November 1899, Churchill was travelling with British troops between Frere and Chieveley in the British Natal Colony when their armoured train was derailed and ambushed by Boer militia. After a brief battle – in which Churchill tried in vain to affect an escape with the driver of the locomotive – he was captured by a Boer Army officer hiding in a ditch (see Old Acquaintance). Churchill's account claims that the Boer soldier raised his rifle to shoot him, and Churchill reached for his pistol – only to discover that he had left it on the train. Unarmed, Churchill had no choice but to surrender.

The British prisoners were marched to a railway siding and transported to Pretoria, where they were held in a converted school that was being used as a POW camp. Churchill spent almost a month at the camp before hitting upon a plan of escape. It should be noted that the plan was hardly complex; nevertheless, it proved to be effective through a mix of brazen daring and good fortune.

Churchill had observed a security lapse during the camp's night watch, so on Tuesday 12 December 1899 he scaled a 3m (10ft) wall and stole his way under the cover of darkness to the railway line. He then stowed away on a goods train heading east. The following day,

hungry and exhausted, Churchill jumped from the train and made his way to the small mining village of Witbank, located 97km (60 miles) from Pretoria. Churchill knocked on the door of the first house he came across to ask for help – by good fortune, he had happened upon the premises of a British-born coal miner named John Howard. The Boer authorities had issued a reward of £25 for Churchill's capture, but Howard agreed to aid his fellow countryman.

Churchill's plan was to reach Lourenço Marques (now Maputo), the capital of Mozambique, where he could contact the British Consulate. So Howard and his associates hid Churchill in a

Churchill arriving in Durban after his escape from Pretoria

mineshaft for three days until a suitable goods train was available, eventually concealing him in carriages full of wool and textiles bound for Mozambique. Churchill finally arrived at his destination, where an associate of Howard's met him from the train and escorted him to the British Consulate. Howard received a telegram on 21 December, stating simply: 'goods arrived safely'.

Churchill's account of his daring escape from the Boer POW camp caused a sensation back in Britain. The *Boy's Own* nature of the story excited the public consciousness, making Churchill a household name overnight. Yet despite, no doubt, enjoying the limelight and all the trappings of his newly found celebrity status, Churchill didn't forget the bravery of the men who had helped him. As tokens of his gratitude, he sent engraved gold watches to Howard and his accomplices.

OLD ACQUAINTANCE

The Boer officer who captured Churchill during the armoured train hijack (see Great Escape) was none other than Louis Botha (1862–1919), the future Prime Minister of the Union of South Africa. Botha, who had been a politician before the Second Boer War broke out, rose through the ranks of the military during

Louis Botha

this conflict on the back of his considerable strategic acumen.

Afterwards, Botha, now Commander-in-Chief of the Transvaal Boers, took part in the Treaty of Vereeniging and attempted to unite a fractured South Africa. In 1902 Botha travelled to London to raise funds for the rebuilding of the Transvaal, where he met and lunched with Churchill. At first Churchill didn't recognize his former captor, but it seems that the two men agreed to let bygones be bygones, becoming firm friends over time.

Botha and Churchill were both involved in the controversial decision to present the Cullinan Diamond to King Edward VII, as a present on the occasion of the monarch's 66th birthday in 1907. Although opinion in South Africa was divided over the fate of the Cullinan, in return for it South Africa received loans to further aid the development of the country. Then, when South Africa received Dominion status in 1910, Botha was the natural choice to become its first Prime Minister.

In his book **Great Contemporaries (1948)**, Churchill wrote in praise of Botha's skills as a military strategist and politician. This could be considered surprising, given that Botha had once been a hair's breadth away from shooting him.

Radical move
Switching from the Conservatives to the Liberals

Churchill's first attempt to enter into politics occurred in 1899 when he contested the by-election for the Oldham constituency seat. Churchill narrowly lost, but he remained undeterred. He tried again at the General Election of 1900, this time securing a narrow victory and winning the seat for the Conservative Party. To celebrate his first political triumph, Churchill set off on a speaking and lecture tour across the UK and parts of North America. The tour turned out to be a popular and lucrative venture: it is estimated that it earned Churchill around £10,000, which roughly equates to around £1 million in today's money.

When Churchill took up his seat in the House of Commons in 1900 as the Member for Oldham, he wasted little time in making his mark. The first four years of his political career were characterized by several high profile disagreements with his own party. At the time the Conservative government were pursuing tariff reform, a series of economic measures intended to protect British industries from the influx of cheap foreign imports, particularly from the colonies. Tariff reform caused a split in the Conservative ranks, and Churchill, as a proponent of free trade, was firmly opposed to any protectionist policies.

Matters came to a head in 1904, which led Churchill to take the radical decision to cross the floor and join the Liberal Party. Although a controversial and bold move for a novice politician to take, this proved to be a shrewd decision – a landslide victory in the 1906 General Election brought the Liberals to government. Having

been effectively deselected by his Oldham constituency, Churchill was invited to stand for the Liberals in the nearby constituency of Manchester North instead.

Common myth
Tonypandy Riots tarnish his reputation

In 1910 Churchill was promoted to the role of Home Secretary in Herbert Henry Asquith's Liberal government. One common myth about Churchill's tenure of this position is that he deployed the army to break up a strike by Welsh miners in 1910. This misconception led to the tarnishing of Churchill's reputation in parts of Wales and in left-wing circles, akin to that of a pantomime villain. However, a recently discovered memo from Churchill to a newspaper editor, believed to date from November 1910, suggests that Churchill was actually extremely reticent about any military intervention in what became a very hostile situation.

Known collectively as the Tonypandy Riots, a series of violent confrontations between the police and striking miners took place in South Wales during the winter of 1910 to 1911. The catalyst for these civil disturbances was a dispute between the owners of the Ely Pit in Penygraig over the speed at which coal was extracted from a newly created coal seam. The mine owners claimed that the miners were on a deliberate 'go-slow'. Meanwhile the miners, for their part, argued that the recently discovered coalface was tricky to mine; also that they were paid by the ton, not by the hour, which meant that it wouldn't be worth their while to be consciously obstructive. After a tit-for-tat exchange of a mine lockout by the owners, followed by a strike by the miners, a deadlock arose in the dispute.

On 6 November 1910, the striking miners learned that the mine owners intended to employ strikebreakers at the Glamorgan Colliery in Llwynypia. The following morning striking miners picketed the Glamorgan Colliery, forming a human shield to thwart and discourage any strikebreakers from entering the colliery. A violent altercation broke out between the police officers placed on duty to protect the strikebreakers and the picketing miners. Further confrontations between the miners and the police continued over the next few days, with the most serious incident taking place on 8 November when the police broke up a demonstration in Tonypandy Square. Rioting ensued, with hundreds of miners and police injured in the ensuing melee.

Fearing an escalation into full-scale civil unrest, Lionel Lindsey, Chief Constable of Glamorgan, contacted the Home Office to request military support. Reluctantly Churchill sent Metropolitan Police reinforcements and some cavalry detachments, but ordered them to hold back and wait in Swindon and Cardiff to monitor developments. When further rioting broke out in Pontypridd on 9 November, a squadron of the 18th Hussars stationed nearby was called in to quell the conflict – but these were not the reinforcements that Churchill had sanctioned.

Police blockade during the miners' strike of 1910 to 1911

Rumours began to circulate in the press that Churchill had ordered the soldiers to use ammunition and fire on the rioters. However Churchill's memo to Alfred Gardiner, Editor of *The Daily News,* refuted this, stating categorically that he had never anticipated the need for the troops to fire on the protestors. Despite clearly showing reluctance to deploy the troops, preferring instead to use their presence as a deterrent rather than brute force, the myth that Churchill used troops against the miners persists in Wales to this day.

Operational command
Controversy over the Siege of Sydney Street

One of the most controversial events in Churchill's early political career concerned his role in the infamous Siege of Sydney Street, which took place in January 1911. On 16 December 1910, police were called to a jeweller's shop in Houndsditch, East London, after a neighbour reported hearing suspicious noises. An immigrant gang of anarchist armed robbers had rented properties adjoining the jeweller's – now it transpired that they were attempting to break into the shop and steal the contents of the safe. In the ensuing melee, three police officers were shot dead and two others were seriously wounded. One of the gang, George Gardstein, was also shot and died the following day from his injuries; the other gang members escaped and went into hiding.

The incident in Houndsditch caused widespread outrage in the press and the East End community, further fuelling the fragile tensions that existed between the locals and immigrants in the area. The police launched an extensive manhunt for the gang, and acting on various tip-offs they were able to apprehend several members. Just after midnight on 3 January 1911 the police, acting on information supplied by an informer, surrounded a property at 100 Sydney Street where two members of the gang were holed up, stationing armed officers behind cordons and barricades. At around 9am a shooting match between the police and the fugitives erupted, which was to last for nearly 6 hours.

As Home Secretary, Churchill was informed of the siege while he was taking his customary morning bath, so he dressed and hurried to the scene. He then gave his consent for the deployment of a detachment of Scots Guards from the Tower of London – a radical decision, as

Churchill at the Siege of Sidney Street in 1911

military forces had never assisted the police in siege situations before. Churchill's role in the operation has since been a matter of some dispute among historians. Shortly after the siege, Churchill wrote in a letter to *The Times* on 12 January 1911: 'I did not interfere in any way with the dispositions made by the police authorities on the spot. I never overruled those authorities nor overrode them. From beginning to end the police had an absolutely free hand… I did not send for the Artillery or the Engineers. I was not consulted as to whether they should be sent for.' However, a report in the Metropolitan Police archives suggests that Churchill's interventions at the siege were an exceptional instance of a Home Secretary making decisions from a police operational command.

At around 1pm in the afternoon on 3 January smoke started to billow from the windows of 100 Sydney Street, gradually taking hold of the building. A chief officer from London's fire brigade requested that he and his men should be allowed to extinguish the fire to avoid damage to nearby properties, but both the police and Churchill refused, expecting to use the fire to 'smoke' the fugitives from the hideout. When the roof subsequently collapsed at around 2.30pm, it became clear that both the men inside the building were dead. The fire brigade were eventually granted permission to douse the flames.

BREAKING NEWS

The Siege of Sydney Street (see Operational Command) was filmed by Pathé News and subsequently broadcast in cinemas, in a sense making it the very first 'breaking news' story of its kind. However, the fact that Churchill was captured on the film footage provided plenty of ammunition for his political opponents in the House of Commons and the press, who viewed it as unbecoming of a Secretary of State to interfere in such matters.

In Parliament, Arthur Balfour, the Leader of the Opposition, seized upon Churchill's involvement as evidence of his

Arthur Balfour

– *Churchill subsequently proposed the introduction of tighter restrictions via a Private Member's Bill. However many of his Liberal Party colleagues objected to Churchill's plans, so they were eventually abandoned.*

Soul mate
Fiercely loyal and devoted wife

An often-overlooked influence on the life of Winston Churchill was the role played by his wife, Clementine 'Clemmie' Hozier (1885–1977). Winston and Clementine were married for 56 years, during which time they endured many ups and downs but remained fiercely loyal and devoted to one another.

Following the death of his father in 1906, Winston appears to have been very eager to start a family of his own – it is thought that he proposed to three different women, all of whom turned him down. Yet in 1908 Winston met Clementine at the dinner party of a mutual acquaintance. Although they had

recklessness and hot-headed approach in moments of crisis. Indeed, Churchill later admitted that perhaps it had been a little foolhardy to be caught on camera. In the aftermath of the siege there was much criticism over the immigration policies of the serving Liberal administration

met briefly before, this time he became entranced by her beauty and lively personality.

After something of a whirlwind romance, the pair was married in St Margaret's Church in Westminster, London, on Tuesday 11 August 1908, barely a month after announcing their engagement. In a short letter to Clementine's mother, Lady Blanche Hozier, asking for her consent to the marriage, Churchill was uncommonly humble in tone, acknowledging that he had little to offer in terms of wealth or position, but nevertheless vowing to make Clementine happy.

In common with Winston, Clementine had experienced an unhappy childhood on account of the tumultuous and public divorce of her parents, and the sudden death of her elder sister, Kitty, from typhoid. Although born of aristocratic stock (she was the granddaughter of David Ogilvy, 10th Earl of Airlie), Clementine found that she was looked down upon by certain segments of high society on account of her family's profligacy with money –

they were forced to move house several times due to rising debts – and her mother's well-known infidelities. As a result, Clementine developed a strong sense of social justice and abhorrence for snobbery and pomposity.

Perhaps surprisingly, given that she was married to a man who twice became a Conservative Prime Minister, Clementine was a liberal through and through, and she wasn't afraid to air her views to Winston in private about some of his more controversial political ideas. During both World Wars, Clementine oversaw valuable charitable work on the home front: in World War I she organized food kitchens for munitions workers; then during World War II she acted as a figurehead for appeal initiatives by the Red Cross and the Young Women's Christian Association.

Clementine was taller than Winston, and considerably more athletic in terms of aptitude and frame. She enjoyed sports and was a strong swimmer, a useful tennis player, and an accomplished equestrian. Her fearlessness is best

Clementine Churchill

Winston's 'Cat', while Winston was Clementine's 'Pug' or 'Pig'.

Although the couple most certainly had their arguments – inevitable when two strong willed people disagree – Winston would often take the role of the appeaser, as he was mindful never to let their disputes linger on or for any resentment to fester.

Clementine's influence upon Winston and his deep respect for her are illustrated in a letter, discovered after his death, that Winston wrote at the Western Front during World War I. As was the practice during the conflict, soldiers wrote sealed letters to be forwarded to their loved ones in event of their death. In this particular letter, Winston expressed in no uncertain terms his deep love and respect for his wife, Clementine. He wrote that she had opened his eyes to the virtues of the female sex, and he pleaded with her not to grieve for him but to love the children and find happiness.

exemplified by her refusal to leave London and her husband's side during the Blitz – as a result, she was given her own bedroom in the Cabinet War Rooms (see Nerve Centre). During periods when the couple were apart they would dutifully write long and affectionate letters to one another, often adorned with little drawings and doodles. They also shared pet names for each other: Clementine was

SHE WHO MUST BE OBEYED

Clementine Churchill, Churchill's wife (see Soul Mate), could be every bit as forthright and stubborn as her notoriously outspoken husband. This was to such an extent that at times, with friends and colleagues, Churchill would refer to her as 'She whose commands must be obeyed'.

While Churchill served as First Lord of the Admiralty between 1911 and 1915, he became deeply involved in developing innovative ideas in warfare technology – most notably the development of tanks and armoured vehicles, and the switch to oil-powered battleships. Churchill was also fascinated by the possibilities of using aeroplane technology and aerial warfare. Ever the daredevil, he even took up flying lessons with the ambition of obtaining a pilot's licence, a move that was firmly at odds with his wife's wishes.

Although Churchill was an enthusiastic pupil who reputedly would beg to be taken up in the air whenever he visited an airfield on official business, flying aeroplanes was considered extremely dangerous at the time. After one of Churchill's flying instructors, Captain Lushington, perished in a plane crash in Kent, Clementine made clear her vehement opposition to her husband's new hobby in a letter, in which she said that every time she received a telegram in his absence she assumed it would inform her of his death in an accident.

Mindful of not causing his wife any further distress, Churchill reluctantly agreed to abandon his plans to become a pilot. He wrote that although it was a hard decision to take, as he'd clearly been bitten by the flying bug, he'd already learned enough to inform any policy decisions that he might have to make in the future relating to the use of aeroplanes in times of war.

'Another boy…'
*Brother Jack's life in
the background*

In his autobiography *My Early Life* (1930), Churchill describes how, during a trip to Switzerland, he saved 'another boy' who was in danger of drowning – which seems rather strange, as the 'boy' was actually his brother. This would naturally lead one to assume that there was animosity between the two, but on the contrary: it appears from the letters they exchanged throughout their lives that Churchill was very fond of his younger sibling.

John Strange Spencer-Churchill (1880–1947), known as Jack, was five years younger than his famous elder brother. Unlike Winston he was academically gifted, hard working and well behaved at school, which led him to be frequently upheld as a shining example by his parents. When their father died in 1895, Winston was 20 and serving with his regiment in India, while 14-year-old Jack was boarding at Harrow School. Randolph

Churchill had, according to their mother Jennie, left no provision for them in his will, other than a small trust fund from which they would only benefit after her death.

This effectively ended Jack's aspirations of a military career, so he was steered by his mother – who, it seems, spent some considerable time and money in advancing Winston's political aspirations – into the stockbroking profession. Jack initially worked as a clerk for Sir Ernest Cassel, an old friend of his family. While thus employed he also joined a part-time regiment, the Oxfordshire Hussars, undertaking his military training at weekends.

At the outbreak of the Second Boer War in 1899, the two brothers joined the South African Light Horse Regiment – Winston was a war correspondent, and Jack was Mentioned in Despatches for his service. Later during World War I, Jack served on the Western Front and at Gallipoli, once again distinguishing himself. He rose to the rank of major before returning to his former employment in the financial sector. Yet this was not before he was awarded the French decorations of the *Croix de Guerre* and the *Legion d'Honneur,* as well as the British Distinguished Service Order.

In 1914 Jack's acumen for figures led him to be tasked with sorting out his mother's divorce from her second husband, George Cornwallis-West. It was then that he discovered she had lied about the content of Randolph's will – their father had, after all, made provision for his sons. In fact, the will entitled Winston and Jack to each draw £600 per annum (around £850,000 in today's money) from the trust on their mother's remarriage – Jennie had deceived them in order to finance her extravagant lifestyle. Considering that Jack had been denied the opportunity to follow his preferred profession, and even had to delay his marriage due to lack of money, he appears to have taken his mother's deception pretty well. Apart from sending her an angry letter on discovering the deceit, he still stayed close to her, as did Winston.

Jack went on to become a successful stockbroker who continued to act as a financial adviser to both his mother and brother – they were both notoriously hopeless with money. Although he never publicly referred to it, Winston's losses caused by the effects of the Wall Street Crash in 1929 and the following Depression could have been considerably worse had it not been for his brother's astute guidance. Widowed in 1941, and then losing his house in the Blitz, Jack was invited by Winston to stay at 10 Downing Street where he occupied the top floor rooms and at one time the annex. During this period he is also known to have assisted the Prime Minister in the Cabinet War Rooms bunker. Jack eventually died in 1947 at the age of 67.

Despite being kept very much in the background, Jack appears to have shown no resentment towards Winston – in fact, the two brothers evidently remained very close. Exactly why Winston chose not to publicly acknowledge the support and encouragement given to him by his younger sibling can only be surmised. Nevertheless, Winston always liked to promote the belief that all his accomplishments had been achieved entirely alone and by his sheer strength of character – Jack's presence, in many ways, would have contradicted this myth.

War strategist
Disaster strikes at Gallipoli

Perhaps Churchill's greatest failure, and certainly an event that haunted him and had a profound effect on his political career, was the disastrous military campaign at Gallipoli during the early months of World War I. When Britain declared war on Germany in the summer of 1914, Churchill held the Cabinet post of First Lord of the Admiralty. Although essentially a political advisory role, the ambitious Churchill, inspired perhaps by his military background and training at Sandhurst, held ambitions as a war strategist.

Churchill became increasingly frustrated at the stalemate in the trenches along the Western Front,

which had claimed the lives of almost a million British and French troops during the first four months of the war alone. Thus on 29 December 1914 Churchill wrote a letter to Prime Minister Herbert Henry Asquith in which he voiced his concerns about the appalling loss of life across the Channel, suggesting that it might be better to open up a new point of attack to avoid the impasse.

Churchill had initially developed a plan to invade Germany via the Baltic Sea. But he now abandoned this idea, instead looking to weaken the coalition of the Central Powers by attempting to knock the Ottoman Empire out of the war. He therefore devised a plan to launch a naval assault in the strait of the Dardanelles, backed up by a land invasion at Gallipoli, with the ultimate goal of capturing Constantinople, which was the capital of the Ottoman Empire.

Churchill believed that establishing a stranglehold on the waterways linking the Mediterranean to the Black Sea would strengthen Britain's alliance with Russia, and force the Germans to reroute resources away from the Western Front. He was in no doubt that the plan was risky, but he felt sure that if the mission was successful it would effectively hasten the end of the conflict.

Thus British warships began a naval assault at the Dardanelles on 19 February 1915. Initially this assault had some success, but a deterioration in the weather delayed further inroads into the strait. On 18 March, several weeks later, a second assault was undertaken. But unbeknown to the British, the Turks had planted mines liberally across the strait – undetected, these sank three British warships and incapacitated several others. Churchill demanded the naval assault to continue but the commander in charge, Admiral John de Robeck, decided to wait for reinforcements before embarking on the land invasion. This hesitation may have been the Allies' undoing, as the month between the naval battle and the eventual attempted landing allowed

The wounded at Gallipoli

the Ottoman army to regroup.

On 25 April, the landing finally took place with a combined force of British, French and Anzac (Australian and New Zealand Army Corps) troops. Having surrendered any element of surprise and having thoroughly underestimated the Turkish resistance, the Battle of Gallipoli rapidly descended into a slaughter and stalemate every bit as futile as the Western Front. In the first month alone the Allies lost thousands of troops, and by the time that the campaign was finally abandoned nine months later, over a quarter of a million Allied and Turkish soldiers had been killed or seriously wounded.

The debacle at Gallipoli caused a political crisis in Britain that ultimately forced Asquith into forming a coalition government with the opposition Conservative Party. Inevitably the search for a scapegoat began, and as the primary architect of the Dardanelles Campaign, blame fell upon the shoulders of Churchill. This is seen by some historians as unfair: Churchill was only really responsible for the naval aspect of the campaign, with the landings falling under the jurisdiction of Field Marshall Lord Kitchener and General Sir Ian Hamilton. It is thought that the Conservatives, still smarting from Churchill's defection from the party a decade earlier, demanded his demotion – as a result, Churchill was replaced as First Lord of the Admiralty and given a peripheral Cabinet role instead.

BRITISH–OTTOMAN ALLIANCE

Although undoubtedly a stain upon Churchill's career as a military strategist (see War Strategist), there is a theory that the disaster of the Gallipoli Campaign may never have occurred if diplomatic relations with the Ottoman Empire hadn't deteriorated during the outbreak of hostilities in World War I. As it turns out, such an alliance may have even been Churchill's goal.

In 1909, Churchill had been invited as a diplomatic guest by the German emperor, Kaiser Wilhelm II, to attend a display of

Ismail Enver Pasha

German army maneuvers. At the subsequent state banquet, Churchill was introduced to the Ottoman Ismail Enver Pasha, a chief figure in the Committee of Union and Progress – Pasha subsequently became the Ottoman Minister of War during World War I. Then in 1910, while on a yachting holiday around the Mediterranean, Churchill docked at Constantinople and held informal meetings with Mehmed Talaat

Pasha, the future Ottoman Grand Vizier and part of the Ottoman ruling triumvirate during World War I, and Mehmed Djavid Bey, the Ottoman Minister of Finance.

Churchill started a correspondence with these high ranking Ottomans, building a relationship that was strong enough for Djavid Bey to contact Churchill to enquire about the possibility of securing British support after the Italian invasion of Libya in 1911. Historians have since speculated that Churchill may have been interested in building a British–Ottoman alliance, but that any suggestion of doing so was dismissed out of hand by the Foreign Secretary of the day, Edward Grey.

On 3 August 1914, as Britain teetered on the brink of World War I, Churchill ordered the requisition of two warships that were under construction in the UK for the Ottoman navy. Churchill was mindful that the ships might be needed if hostilities with Germany escalated, so he wrote to Enver Pascha to explain his decision and *to offer payment to the Ottomans for their use. Naturally the Ottomans didn't take kindly to their ships being 'borrowed', which is sometimes cited as a contributing factor in the deterioration of British–Ottoman relations. However, unbeknown to Churchill at the time, the Ottomans had already signed a secret alliance with Germany, just the day before the ships were requisitioned. The following day Germany invaded Belgium, forcing Britain, somewhat reluctantly, to enter the conflict.*

Therapeutic hobby
Development of a landscape artist

The failure of the Dardanelles expedition in 1915 (see War Strategist) was to haunt Churchill, and the event resulted in his relegation to the minor position of Chancellor of the Duchy of Lancaster at the end of that year. Feeling bored in his new job, Churchill joined the army as a lieutenant colonel and found himself placed in command of the 6th Battalion of the Royal Scots Fusiliers. While he was waiting for a call to embark to France and the Western Front of World War I, Churchill took up painting as a hobby. He wrote that he came across a child's painting set at home and started daubing a few pictures as a way to relax and calm the anxieties of his political life. Churchill then invested in a set of oils with a view to teaching himself how to paint landscapes.

It was during World War I that Churchill met the French-born artist Paul Maze (1887–1979), who was serving in an unofficial capacity as a draughtsman for the British Army. Maze was initially employed as an interpreter, but he also undertook dangerous reconnaissance work, sneaking into No Man's Land to produce detailed plans and maps of enemy positions. No doubt impressed by Maze's bravery and artistic skills, Churchill became close friends with the artist – indeed Maze was to become Churchill's artistic mentor, actively encouraging

Churchill painting in 1946

him in his newfound hobby.

Churchill continued to paint after the war: in 1925 he won a prize in an amateur artists' competition for his painting *Winter Sunshine, Chartwell,* and over the next 50 years he produced over 500 paintings – mostly landscapes, but also still lifes and interior scenes. Maze would often accompany Churchill on painting holidays, and many of Churchill's works were depictions of scenes from trips that they made to France, Italy and Morocco. In terms of style, Churchill's landscapes show a leaning towards Impressionism: this may have been influenced by Maze, who is regarded as one of the last Impressionists. Churchill was also known to be an ardent admirer of Monet, Cézanne and Turner.

Although Churchill entered his paintings into competitions and offered his paintings for exhibition in Paris and at the Royal Academy, he often used the pseudonyms 'Charles Morin' or 'Mr Winter' in his applications – he wished his art to be judged on its own merits and not on the basis of his fame. Churchill was also reticent to exhibit his paintings in an exhibition of his own, preferring to keep them private and occasionally presenting them to close friends as gifts.

However, in 1958 the American entrepreneur J. C. Hall managed to persuade Churchill to send 35 paintings to the USA to be exhibited at the Nelson Gallery in Kansas City where Hall lived. Churchill and Hall were acquainted (see Season's Greetings) and the Kansas exhibition turned out to be a great success. Hall had a sharp eye for a business opportunity, so he then hurriedly arranged for the exhibition to tour some of the USA's most prestigious museums and galleries, including the Smithsonian Institute and the Metropolitan Museum of Modern Art in New York. Wherever the paintings went, huge crowds gathered to see them, although Churchill was heard to comment at the time that this was largely due to his fame and notoriety in the USA, rather than the artistic merit of the work.

Churchill was more than an enthusiastic amateur, although because he came to painting relatively late in life he hadn't the time to develop his artistic skills properly. More importantly perhaps, Churchill used painting as a release and an escape, especially during times of depression (see Black Dog) – he highly valued the therapeutic aspect of his artistic endeavours. Towards the end of his life Churchill wrote, in a rather jocular fashion, that he intended to devote his time in heaven to the art of painting.

Today, Churchill's paintings are highly sought-after by collectors and exhibited in various galleries and museums around the world. In 2015, following the death of Churchill's daughter, Mary, 37 of Churchill's more notable paintings were given to the National Trust for display in the garden studio at his former home of Chartwell in Kent.

SEASON'S GREETINGS

Joyce Clyde Hall (1891–1982; see Therapeutic Hobby), known as J. C. Hall, was the founder of the Hallmark greetings card empire. Hall first met Churchill on 5 March 1946 when Hall visited Westminster College in Fulton, Missouri, to hear Churchill deliver his now famous 'Iron Curtain' speech denouncing the Soviet Union; the two men were introduced at a special reception for civic guests after the speech. Hall then read Churchill's book **Painting as a Pastime** *(1948), so he hit upon the idea of reproducing some of Churchill's paintings on Hallmark greetings cards. Hall instructed his company solicitors to approach Churchill, and to everyone's surprise he agreed to the proposal – it seems that Churchill was quite amused at the prospect of his paintings appearing as Christmas card designs.*

Churchill duly shipped 12 paintings over to the USA to be photographed. Their arrival in Kansas City, Missouri, happened to coincide with a conference of museum directors and curators, so Hall hastily arranged a private view for prominent conference delegates – it was at this point that he hit upon the idea of exhibiting Churchill's works. As it turned out, Churchill's Christmas cards proved to be among Hallmark's top-selling cards over the next few years, and as a result Hall and his family were invited to visit Churchill at his home of Chartwell when they visited Europe in 1950. Hall and Churchill became friends who regularly corresponded and met several times.

Although Churchill resisted Hall's idea for an exhibition for several years, Hall remained unperturbed. He persisted in his goal, even enlisting the help of President Eisenhower in trying to persuade Churchill to change his mind. Meanwhile the friendship between the Churchill and Hall family continued to blossom, with J. C. Hall inviting Churchill's daughter, the actress Sarah Churchill, to host her own chat show programme on the NBC

Television Network, sponsored by Hallmark. Eventually Churchill relented and agreed to the US exhibition – and he was delighted with the outcome. Hall and Churchill met for the last time in 1964, a year before Churchill's death. Hall notes in his memoir **When You Care Enough** *(1979) that Churchill spoke warmly of the times they had spent together, and thanked him for arranging the exhibition.*

Publically accused
Allegations of Lord Alfred Douglas

In 1923 Churchill was publically accused of using his political position as a Cabinet minister during World War I to falsify an official report on the Battle of Jutland in order to manipulate international stock market prices. Lord Alfred Douglas (1870–1945) made the allegations, a man who had reached notoriety through his controversial friendship with Oscar Wilde in the 1890s. Douglas had since gained a reputation for his involvement in litigious lawsuits, having been both a plaintiff and a defendant in a number of trials for civil and criminal libel.

An open anti-Semite, Douglas claimed in his journal *Plain English* and also at a public meeting that Churchill was in the pay of a group of Jewish financiers, which included Sir Ernest Cassel. He suggested that Churchill had influenced the government's announcement of the naval defeat at Jutland that had caused British stocks to collapse in return

Oscar Wilde and Alfred Douglas

for a house full of fine furniture. Douglas went on to claim that Churchill had subsequently publically stated that the battle was not in fact a total rout, which caused share prices to rebound and enabled his Jewish associates, who had bought low and sold high, to make huge financial gains.

In his claims, Douglas even went so far as to infer that Churchill had actually played a part in arranging

the death of Field Marshall Lord Kitchener, who had been killed in 1916 aboard HMS *Hampshire* when the ship struck a mine west of the Orkney Isles. The Kitchener story made for good reading, and the pamphlet in which the story was published sold 6,000 copies over two days in London alone. Churchill subsequently sued for libel.

The incidents cited by Douglas had actually occurred, but when the case came to trial it emerged that the Earl of Balfour was in fact the author of the infamous Jutland communiqué, and that Churchill had taken no part in drafting the document. It was also revealed that Churchill was asked by the government to issue the statement that claimed Jutland had not been a total defeat in order to boost public morale. And in court, it transpired that the source of Lord Alfred's claim regarding Kitchener's death was that of a bogus sea captain who was also a certified lunatic.

With regard to Sir Ernest Cassel, who had died by the time of the court case, his confidential secretary testified that other than subscribing large amounts to the British war loan, at the time of the alleged incident Cassel had no dealings of any kind with the British stock market. It was also well known that Cassel had been a good friend of Churchill's father, Randolph, and had known Winston since his childhood. While giving evidence in court, Churchill stated that the only gifts he had ever been given by Cassel were furniture for one room in a house that he had rented in 1905, along with a cheque for £500 when he married Clementine in 1908.

Eventually Lord Alfred Douglas was found guilty of libel and sentenced to six months of imprisonment. However, he evidently felt no ill will towards Churchill: in 1940 he wrote a poem to the then Prime Minister, praising him and wishing him well in his wartime leadership. Churchill, in return, accepted this praise with magnanimity.

BARBED RIPOSTES

Initially at least, Churchill was opposed to the women's suffrage movement. It is therefore perhaps no surprise that some of his most famous and barbed ripostes were directed at Lady Nancy Astor (1879–1964), the first woman to take up a seat in Parliament. In response to accusations by Lady Astor at a party that he was

Nancy Astor

slurring his words and clearly drunk, Churchill is alleged to have replied: 'Yes Madam, but in the morning I will be sober but you will still be ugly.' On another occasion at a dinner party, in relation to Lady Astor suggesting that Churchill's wife was a saint for putting up with him, she is said to have remarked: 'If you were my husband I would poison your coffee.' To which Churchill supposedly drolly replied: 'Madam, if I were your husband I would drink it.'

Yet Churchill didn't always get the better of Nancy Astor. During a debate in Parliament on agricultural policy, Churchill allegedly stood up to challenge a contribution made by Lady Astor: 'I venture to say that my Right Honorable friend, so redolent of other knowledge, knows nothing of farming. I'll even make a bet that she doesn't know how many toes a pig has.' Unfazed, Lady Astor is said to have replied that she did in fact know how many toes a pig had because she had seen Churchill without his shoes on.

'Cosy pig'
Chartwell becomes home

'A day away from Chartwell is a day wasted' is a quote often cited and sums up the love that Churchill had for the country home, set in 80 acres of land, which he purchased in 1922 and lived in on and off for the rest of his life. Nicknamed 'cosy pig' by Churchill, it is sited 3km (2 miles) from the town of Westerham in Kent, and only 40km (25 miles) from central London. Chartwell thus provided an ideal location for Churchill to travel to the capital in order to carry out his parliamentary affairs, as well as a convenient location for the many famous houseguests he entertained.

On their 14th wedding anniversary, Clementine, Churchill's wife, had written a letter to her husband in which she expressed her wish for a house in the country in order to bring 'great happiness and peace in our lives.' The very next day Churchill made an offer of £4,800 for Chartwell; the owners at the time, the Campbell Colquhouns, had been asking

£5,500 for the property, but Churchill insisted that there was dry rot so extensive work was needed to make it habitable – they finally agreed on a price of £5,000. Unfortunately Churchill was proved right, and the couple could not actually move into the property until 1924 when renovations had been completed.

Despite attaining the country home she had yearned for, Clementine's desire to live within their means was never realized –

although money was tight, Churchill went ahead and employed the services of the architect Philip Tilden. At the time, Tilden worked exclusively for the rich and famous in English society, being able to list among his clients David Lloyd George, Lord Beaverbrook, Sir Philip Sassoon, Lady Ottoline Morrell and Gordon Selfridge. Tilden worked for two years on Chartwell, retaining its period features but adding larger windows and more rooms. In fact, the house

Chartwell in Kent

was extended to five reception rooms, 19 bed- and dressing rooms, and eight bathrooms.

Records show that there had been a property named Chartwell on the site as early as 1362, its name deriving from the old English word 'chart', which means rough ground, and the well to be found in the grounds. However, the original timbers, some of which are still present, date the current building to between 1515 and 1546: Chartwell is likely to have been constructed as a hunting lodge, where King Henry VIII reputedly stayed during his courtship of Anne Boleyn, who was living 8km (5 miles) away at Hever Castle. In the 1700s Chartwell was renamed Well Street and was used as the Westerham branch of the London Foundling Hospital, an institution founded by the philanthropist Thomas Coram for the 'education and maintenance of exposed and deserted young children.' In 1836 it was sold to the Drinkwater Bethune family from Surrey, and eventually to the Campbell Colquhouns, who renamed the house Chartwell.

FAVOURITE PASTIMES

In his later years, Churchill claimed that he had bought Chartwell (see 'Cosy Pig') for its impressive views over the Weald of Kent. In the early 1930s when he no longer had a position in the government, Churchill spent most of his time at Chartwell, working on books and newspaper articles. It was during this period that Churchill found time to devote to his love of painting – which he claimed brought him some relief from his bouts of depression – and the commanding scenery to be viewed from the property was the subject of many of his works. In fact, he converted a cottage in the grounds into an art studio, where he produced around 500 paintings over the course of his lifetime.

Apart from painting, Churchill's other favourite pastime was bricklaying. He was obviously very accomplished at this, as is evidenced by the intricate walls and small buildings he constructed around the Chartwell estate – his work includes various brick outbuildings, a swimming pool, and the wall that borders the vegetable garden. Churchill boasted that he laid 200 bricks and wrote 2,000 words a day – there is even a plaque on a wall that winds around the estate stating that it was built 'by Winston with his own hands', largely between 1925 and 1932. In fact, Churchill was so proficient at bricklaying that he became a card-carrying member of the Amalgamated Union of Building Trade Workers – extremely unusual for a member of the Conservative Party.

Under threat
Chartwell at risk

Never a man to live within his means (see High Life), by 1938 Churchill found himself in financial trouble. His books and articles proved to generate insufficient income to maintain the house and the lifestyle to which he was accustomed, therefore he was forced to consider selling Chartwell – and he actually got as far as advertising it. Fortunately for him, Sir Henry Strakosch, a banker and businessman, agreed to take over Churchill's share portfolio, thus enabling him to take the property off the market.

During World War II it became impossible for the Churchills to stay at Chartwell due to its close proximity to the English Channel, which made it extremely vulnerable to attack both from the air and by possible Nazi commando raids. Therefore the family spent most of the war in Oxfordshire, and later at the official Prime Minister's residence at Chequers in Buckinghamshire.

Once more, in 1946 the Churchills' life at Chartwell appeared to be under threat, again from Winston's unhealthy financial situation. Happily a group of his wealthy friends, headed by Lord Camrose, intervened. They purchased the estate with the proviso that the Churchills paid a nominal rent for the duration of their tenure, and that it was left to the National Trust after the deaths of both Winston and Clementine. In the event, Clementine handed over Chartwell to the National Trust within just a year of her husband's death.

Today, Chartwell still receives thousands of visitors each year. The visitor's book on a side table in the hall records the names of every guest who stayed there and enjoyed Churchill's hospitality, including: David Lloyd George, Lawrence of Arabia, Harry Truman, Field Marshall Montgomery and Charlie Chaplin. Some of the guest accommodation has now been turned into museum rooms, but for the most part the house has been restored to reflect its heydays of the 1930s. However, Churchill's study has been allowed to remain very much as he himself had left it.

Charlie Chaplin

Animal lover
Surrounding himself with pets

Churchill was very much an animal lover, and during his life he surrounded himself with pets – many given to him as gifts, and some exotic. Apart from dogs, cats, a budgie, pigs, poultry and sheep, he kept goldfish and Golden Orfe at Chartwell, and was gifted two pairs of black swans – the first pair by Philip Sassoon, and the second by the Government of Western Australia. He also built a butterfly house, and at one time even explored the possibility of keeping kangaroos on his estate. In 1943 Churchill was presented with a lion called Rota: for obvious reasons, he was unable to look after this himself, but he regularly visited the creature at its home in London Zoo.

Churchill's idea that his family should live off the land when they moved to Chartwell proved financially unsuccessful. In part, this was due to Churchill's distaste at the thought of slaughtering livestock, but also his resistance to modern

Miniature poodle

farming methods – he simply could not contemplate the idea of his animals being artificially inseminated, insisting that his beasts would not be deprived. Indeed, on one occasion when a Chartwell goose was served for dinner, Churchill allegedly asked his wife to carve the bird, as he couldn't face cutting up 'a friend of mine'.

In 1947 Churchill was distraught when a car killed Rufus, his chocolate-brown miniature poodle, who had become the Prime Minister's constant companion during World War II. Shortly afterward, Churchill replaced Rufus with a similar looking dog, which he named Rufus II. They remained together until 1962 when the poodle died peacefully in his sleep.

Throughout his life Churchill always kept cats, which he would allow into the dining room during mealtimes and sneakily feed when he thought his wife's attention was elsewhere. His favourite wartime feline was a large grey cat that he adopted after seeing it chase a huge dog out of the Admiralty building – he named the cat Nelson because of its bravery. It is said that Nelson did his bit for the war effort by keeping the Prime Minister warm in his bed at night, thus saving on coal. Nelson subsequently moved into 10 Downing Street with Churchill, where there was already a cat in residence that Churchill named the Munich Mouser, being a relic from the previous Chamberlain administration. There were reportedly several spats between the two animals before the brave Nelson finally chased his adversary permanently from the property.

At Chartwell during the 1930s, an occasion is recorded where Churchill flapped his newspaper and shouted at one of the many cats that resided there over the years. The cat in question scooted out of the door and was not seen for several days. Churchill was troubled by this, instructing his secretary to put a card in the window to inform the cat that all was forgiven. Unbeknown to Churchill, the poor creature had met with an accident, but was eventually returned and treated to cream and the best salmon to assist its recovery.

Later in life, Churchill's love of animals also led him to develop an interest in horseracing. He therefore embarked on a highly successful career as an owner and breeder, with his racehorse Colonist II winning many victories for the statesman (see Glittering Career).

JOCK THE CAT

Churchill was notoriously fond of pets (see Animal Lover). Thus in 1962 Jock Colville, Churchill's private secretary and close friend, presented him with a ginger cat with a white chest and white paws – the cat immediately became a close companion. His master named him Jock and the cat was always seen sitting on Churchill's knee. Jock travelled by car with Churchill on his visits to their London residence at Hyde Park Gate, and in a photograph of Churchill leaving his London home to attend Parliament for the final time Jock can be seen in the foreground.

When the family finally handed Chartwell over to the National Trust in 1966, they requested that a marmalade cat with a white chest and white socks remain in residence. The National Trust obliged, so the original Jock enjoyed the run of the house until his death in 1975 at the age of 13. The current incumbent is named Jock IV and resides in an apartment

Jock, the current resident at Chartwell

at Chartwell with a member of staff. He, too, has the run of the grounds – he can even boast his own cat flap, which has been approved by the Historic Buildings Inspector and is painted in National Trust Green.

Hobby and habit
Passion for smoking cigars

During his stay in Cuba at the age of 19 Churchill developed a passion for Cuban cigars, but cigar smoking is a habit that appears to have begun much earlier. While attending Harrow School at the age of 15, his mother begged Churchill to refrain from the habit, at least for a few years – not on health grounds, but because she felt it made him look foolish. She eventually resorted to bribery, promising him a gun and a pony if he would stop for six months. Churchill successfully took up his mother's challenge, then promptly resumed the habit – after, one supposes, he had received the promised gifts.

Typically, Churchill worked his way through an average of ten cigars a day, although he did not constantly smoke them, often leaving a cigar to burn out and then just chewing on it. Ever inventive, he overcame the problem of soggy cigars by devising a tool called the bellybando, which was simply a strip of brown paper glued around a cigar end. Also, rather than using a cigar cutter – of which he collected many over the years – Churchill imported extra-long matches from Canada. After moistening the end of a cigar then poking a hole through it with one of these matches, he blew from the other end to ensure that the cigar would draw properly.

Churchill was almost inseparable from his prized silver pagoda-shaped ashtray: wherever he travelled this was packed in its special case then taken along too. The said ashtray would also accompany him to hotels and restaurants, where it would be handed to the headwaiter to be ceremoniously brought out after dinner. Despite this, Churchill was notorious for leaving a trail of cigar ash on carpets, and also for burning holes in his suits – as a consequence, these were regularly sent away for repair. In an attempt to save her husband's expensive silk pyjamas from being singed, Clementine created a special bib for him to wear while smoking in bed.

Although he was regularly presented with cigars, Churchill's ten-a-day habit meant that he regularly had to purchase them himself – usually from his favourite cigar merchant, Fox's, which is still trading today in St James, London. Unsurprisingly, over the years he spent a good deal of money on this habit: in fact, one of his valets later revealed that the money Churchill spent on cigars in two days equated to his own weekly wage.

Churchill's favourite cigars were the Cuban brands Romeo y Julieta and La Aroma de Cuba. But he did not restrict himself to these, keeping a collection of between 3,000 to 4,000 cigars of various sizes and makes (mostly gifts) in a room adjacent to his study at Chartwell,

categorized by size and whether they were wrapped or unwrapped. In 1941, when presented with 2,400 cigars by Fulgencio Batista, the President of Cuba, Churchill's security team ensured that one from each box was analysed for poison – understandably so, as this was at the height of World War II.

RIGHT TO SMOKE

Churchill appeared to believe that it was his right to smoke his cigars (see Hobby and Habit) anywhere he chose simply because of his renown, and this was evidently tolerated – the only person allowed to smoke in the presence of Field Marshall Montgomery was Churchill. This was further borne out in 1945 when Churchill hosted a luncheon in honour of King Ibn Sa'ud of Saudi Arabia. In his war memoirs, Churchill recalled that he was informed that it would be a problem if anyone smoked or drank alcohol in the royal presence. Yet after an interpreter told King Ibn that Churchill's rule of life 'prescribed, as an absolutely sacred

Churchill smoking a cigar

Remarkably, this request was accommodated and he managed to puff on a cigar at an altitude of 4,500m (15,000ft) through a special hole in his oxygen mask.

Gold standard
Grave political misjudgement

Field Marshall Montgomery

rite, smoking cigars and also the drinking of alcohol before, after and, if need be, during all meals and in the intervals between them', the king accepted the situation.

Churchill's determination to smoke anywhere also became evident prior to him taking his first high-altitude flight in an unpressurized cabin. As he was fitted for a flight suit and an oxygen mask the day before, Churchill requested that a mask be designed that enabled him to smoke his cigars while airborne.

Churchill lost his seat in Parliament at the 1922 General Election when he stood again for the constituency of Dundee: falling ill during the election campaign, he had undergone an appendectomy operation that had seriously hampered his campaign. World War I had also taken its toll on Churchill's reputation (see War Strategist), and he was struggling to maintain his pre-war profile as a political statesman. Deeming it time for a short sabbatical, Churchill therefore decamped to the South of France to concentrate on writing and painting.

In 1924, now standing as an independent under the loose term of a 'constitutionalist', Churchill was returned to Parliament as the Member for Epping. Yet internal divisions within the Liberal Party and Churchill's disgust at the Liberals' support for the Labour government led Churchill once again to switch his political allegiances – he re-joined the Conservatives. Invited by Prime Minister Stanley Baldwin to take a seat on the Cabinet, Churchill eagerly accepted the position of Chancellor of the Exchequer.

In his first budget as Chancellor, Churchill took the decision to return Britain to the gold standard, a fixed exchange rate mechanism that had been suspended during World War I. On 28 April 1925 Churchill announced this decision, which was met with loud cheers in the House of Commons. Churchill himself had reservations about the wisdom of fixing the value of currency at pre-war levels, but advice from financial institutions

The Bank of England

such as the Treasury and the Bank of England forced his hand. The theory was that London needed to re-establish itself as a global financial stronghold, which was viewed as the only way to return the nation to pre-war prosperity.

The move proved to be an economic disaster: the fixed exchange rate caused British industry to become uncompetitive and the sterling currency to find itself vulnerable to global market forces. British trade had suffered in the 1920s: firstly, because British industries had failed to keep up with modern developments after the war; then because the shift from coal to oil had a devastating effect on the coal industry, leading to the General Strike of 1926. Subsequently unemployment rose dramatically and the rise in interest rates necessitated by maintaining the strength of the currency when linked to the gold standard affected businesses large and small. Ultimately the rapid decline of Britain's core industries such as coal and cotton served as prelude to the Great Depression that followed the Wall Street Crash of 1929.

Churchill came to regard the return to the gold standard as one of his greatest political misjudgements, although in hindsight it seems that he was only guilty of taking bad advice from financial experts, perhaps because he felt uncertain of his competence in his new role as Chancellor. This is a rare example of Churchill failing to follow his own instincts, as he had spent several months agonizing over the decision to return to the pre-war exchange rate mechanism. The gold standard was finally abandoned in the UK in 1931.

Meanwhile, in the USA the gold standard was also abandoned in 1933 during the height of the Great Depression – yet it still remains a moot point in economic theory. In 2012, the libertarian Republican senator Ron Paul suggested in a speech to Congress that the US economy would greatly benefit from a return to the gold standard – a radical position in the face of over 80 years of economic zeitgeist.

EDITOR-IN-CHIEF

When the General Strike broke out on 3 May 1926 (see Gold Standard), the UK ground to a virtual standstill. The printing unions also supported the strike, which meant that newspapers, the main source of information distribution at the time, were either not produced, or produced in a very short and flimsy form.

As a leading member of the government, Churchill took the unprecedented decision to commandeer the printing presses of **The Morning Post,** *a traditional daily newspaper with right-wing leanings, as the official government mouthpiece in order to spread anti-strike propaganda. At the time a noted former journalist, Churchill installed himself as Editor-in-Chief of the paper, renaming it* **The British Gazette.**

In the absence of any competition from its dormant competitors and a virtual news blackout, **The British Gazette** *garnered a wide circulation – this rapidly increased from 200,000*

The British Gazette

copies for its fledgling edition to almost 2 million when the paper ceased publication at the end of the strike on 13 May. In total, Churchill presided over eight editions of **The British Gazette,** *which are now enthusiastically traded on online auction sites by collectors of Churchill memorabilia.*

Black dog
Struggles with depression

The expression 'black dog' refers to depression, and is commonly associated with Churchill as he used it throughout his life – in fact many believe it to be one of the many terms coined by the man himself. However this is not the case: the expression seems to have much older origins, and similar euphemisms have been used for generations across other languages and cultures.

In several 19th-century dictionaries the phrase is used to refer to a sulky child, 'he had a black dog on his back', or as a description for general melancholia. And reportedly Mrs Everest, Churchill's nanny, used to describe him as 'having a black dog on his shoulder' when he was in a black mood, which does seem to be the most likely reason for Churchill's reference to it throughout his life. Meanwhile, in 20th-century dictionaries the term came to be associated with the condition known as delirium tremens, relating to alcohol withdrawal.

Churchill experienced bouts of depression from a relatively young age. The episodes would sometimes last for several months, causing him to lose interest in the world around him and stop talking to people – subsequently, the accompanying symptoms of fatigue combined with loss of appetite would drive him to his bed. On occasions, the black dog would appear when Churchill had experienced a traumatic event: for example, after his demotion from the post of First Lord of the Admiralty in 1915, as a consequence of the disastrous Dardanelles Campaign (see War Strategist).

Lord Moran

However, this was not always the case – some episodes seem to have materialized for no apparent external reason. In 1911, Churchill excitedly wrote to Clementine, his wife, on hearing that a friend's wife had been helped to deal with her depression by a German doctor. Unfortunately at the time, little was known about the causes of depression, and there was no medication available to control the illness. Lord Moran, his personal physician from 1940, described Churchill's symptoms in his memoirs but was unable to suggest any treatment.

When untroubled by 'the dog', Churchill experienced phenomenal amounts of energy, and was able to combine his parliamentary duties with prolific writing – during his lifetime he produced more words than Shakespeare and Dickens put together – often functioning on as little as four hours of sleep a night. When all was well, Churchill was full of confidence and on top of the world. In later life, Churchill seems to have worked out how to control his black dog to some extent by throwing himself into his favourite pastimes of bricklaying and painting (see Favourite Pastimes), alongside his continued copious output of articles and books.

MANIC DEPRESSION

From what is known of his depression (see Black Dog), some experts have now asserted that Churchill was probably suffering from manic depression, similar to what we now label as bipolar disorder. They point to well-known Churchillian traits that appear to fit, at least partially, with the bipolar pattern:

- *An unwavering sense of self-importance and belief in his grand destiny.*
- *Seemingly, an inability to plan or keep track of his finances, coupled with a penchant for gambling.*
- *His abnormally high energy levels.*
- *A lack of inhibition that is well documented – for example, dictating to his secretaries from*

his bed, meeting people dressed in only a bathrobe or even in his bath, and often walking around his home naked.

- *His obsessive and seemly inexhaustible writing.*
- *A confrontational personality.*

Whatever the exact nature of Churchill's mental condition, for a man who avoided standing too close to the edge of railway platforms while trains were passing, and who felt uneasy when looking into the water from the side of a ship, Churchill's temperament stood him in good stead when he commanded Britain in what would have appeared to most leaders of a more rational disposition as an unwinnable war.

High life
Struggles with money

Churchill came from a background of considerable wealth and privilege, which was reflected in his desire to maintain a luxurious lifestyle. However, it appears that he did not have a natural gift for managing his finances. In 1939, the year before his election to the position of Prime Minister, Churchill had amassed an overdraft of £35,000 (£2 million in today's money) and was being chased by his brokers for an immediate payment of £12,000 (£720,000 today). Fortunately for Churchill, a group of benefactors concerned that he was about to be elected to lead Britain into a war in Europe settled his debts on his behalf.

Yet Churchill's propensity for the finer things in life had been causing a build-up of debt for many years. Despite numerous attempts to curb his extravagancies, it appears that Churchill continued spending in the same vein throughout his life. For example, in his 30s, despite being a married man and responsible for a young family of four children, it is well documented that he was borrowing the equivalent of £2.5 million today. A large percentage of Churchill's borrowings were spent on gambling and alcohol. Moreover, he would think nothing of squandering what amounted to around £40,000 today on annual holidays to the South of France, during which he would visit the local casinos. It is reputed that a friend once bet Churchill that he could not cut down on his drinking – never a man to turn down a wager, Churchill managed to curb his expenditure on alcohol for that year to £900 (£54,000 today).

Other examples of Churchill's extravagance include his habit of smoking 10 to 12 cigars a day – this alone cost him £1,300 per month at that time. Meanwhile, during a period of two months in 1949, Churchill and his numerous houseguests at Chartwell managed to consume 454 bottles of champagne, 311 bottles of wine, 69 bottles of port, 58 bottles of brandy, 58 bottles of sherry and 56 bottles of Black Label whisky. These excesses evidently continued throughout his life. In fact, while the rest of Britain was restricted by rationing, Churchill continued to enjoy the good life, socializing with world leaders at high society parties.

OUTSTANDING BILLS

In 2015, Churchill's tailors of many years made their records available to the public. This led to the revelation that in 1937 Churchill had left an outstanding bill with Henry Poole & Co. of Savile Row that amounted to £197 (over £12,000 in today's money).

Churchill first visited Henry Poole & Co. as a young man of 20 in 1905. He continued to use the services of this business for over 30 years, commissioning it to make all his clothes, including the formal apparel for his positions as Under Secretary of State for the Colonies, Privy Councillor, President of the Board of Trade, Home Secretary, First Lord of the Admiralty, Secretary of State for War, Chancellor of the Exchequer,

David Lloyd George and Winston Churchill wearing tailored apparel in 1907

and as an Elder Brother of Trinity House. However Churchill proved to be an infrequent payer – other businesses such as his butcher and florist apparently also had difficulty obtaining their money from him. Eventually in 1939, unbeknown to the owner, a clerk working for the tailoring company sent a letter to Churchill that demanded payment for the outstanding amount.

Churchill was affronted by this request. According to the company records, he 'took umbrage and quit' their patronage, claiming that it was as good for 'morale' as it was for Henry Poole & Co.'s business for him to be well dressed, and that 'he wasn't aware that they were short of money'. The proprietor was extremely upset by this 'falling out', but there are no records of the fate of the clerk who had initiated the incident.

However, at that time it was not unusual for wealthy clients to leave their bills unpaid. According to the accounts of Henry Poole & Co.: the future King Edward VII 'made infrequent payments on his account that accumulated over the years'; the actress Lillie Langtry ran up large sums with the company; and Charles Dickens had to clear a substantial debt that had been accrued by his son. Many historians talk about a motto of sorts among the wealthy, along the lines of 'You pay your doctor, your dentist but you never pay your tailor.'

Prolific output
Remarkable literary endeavours

Winston Churchill's main claim to fame is, of course, being the Prime Minister who led Britain to victory in World War II. Yet if fate had taken a different turn and another politician had seized the helm, Churchill would still have been, to a somewhat lesser extent, renowned as a famous author and the recipient of a Nobel Prize for Literature, which he accepted in 1953 for his six-volume work, *The Second World War*. During the course of his life, Churchill wrote 43 works in 72 volumes of fiction and non-fiction, as well as hundreds of articles.

By the age of 26 Churchill had already published six books and had become one of the highest paid journalists in Britain. While working as a reporter in the Second Boer War, he was earning £250 per month (£10,000 in today's money); in 1903, when he was commissioned to write an account of his father's life, he received the considerable sum of £8,000 (£320,000 in today's money). The reason Churchill was so well paid was because he was already a popular figure with the public and publishers knew that his work would sell. But he was also a very talented and accomplished writer, who knew how to hold the reader's attention.

While out of government in the 1930s, Churchill relied – not always successfully – on his writing to bring in enough money to run Chartwell and maintain his extravagant lifestyle (see High Life). In order to do this, he sometimes had to accept work that he would not normally have considered. For instance, during the period from 1932 to 1933, he was contracted by *The News of the World* to write a series of articles entitled *Great Stories of the World Retold* that were abbreviated re-writes of classic novels. Although somewhat lightweight in comparison to his usual works, these proved to be quite lucrative, earning him £333 per article and helping to keep his creditors at bay.

It was typical for Churchill, a man

of unusual energy, to commence work on his manuscripts at around 10pm, solidly dictating to his secretary for often up to six hours at a time and producing around 2,000 words a day. After his words were typed up, he would scrutinize them and make amendments in ink then the corrected version would be re-typed. Once the printer had typeset the work, Churchill would make further changes until he was totally satisfied, before sending the work back for final setting. This was an expensive and time-consuming process – but Churchill was a perfectionist.

Amazingly, Churchill was able to sustain this prolific output while conducting his political duties. Including all of his history books, journalism, essays, speeches and pamphlets, it is estimated that Churchill wrote over 10 million words during his lifetime. A list of his works is as follows, with the dates of each publication given in brackets afterwards:

Non-fiction

*The Story of the Malakand Field
    Force (*1898)
The River War (1899)

The River War

*London to Ladysmith via
    Pretoria* (1900)
Ian Hamilton's March (1900)
Lord Randolph Churchill (1906)
My African Journey (1908)
The World Crisis (1923–31)
    (6 vols)
My Early Life (1930)
Thoughts and Adventures (1932)

Marlborough: His Life and Times
   (1933–38) (4 vols)
Great Contemporaries (1937)
The Second World War
   (1948–1953) (6 vols)
Painting as a Pastime (1948)
A History of the English-Speaking
   Peoples (1956–1958) (4 vols)

Fiction
Savrola (1898)
The Dream (1947)

Collected books of
Churchill's speeches
Mr Broderick's Army (1903)
For Free Trade (1906)
Liberalism and the Social
   Problem (1909)
The People's Rights (1910)
Parliamentary Government and the
   Economic Problem (1930)
India: Speeches and an
   Introduction (1931)
Arms and the Covenant (1938)
Step by Step: 1936–1939 (1939)
Addresses Delivered (1940)
Into Battle (1941)
Broadcast Addresses (1941)
The Unrelenting Struggle (1942)

The End of the Beginning (1943)
Winston Churchill, Prime
   Minister (1943)
Onwards to Victory (1944)
The Dawn of Liberation (1945)
Victory (1946)
Secret Sessions Speeches (1946)
War Speeches (1946)
World Spotlight Turns on
   Westminster (1946)
The Sinews of Peace (1946)
Europe Unite: Speeches 1947 and
   1950 (1951)
The War Speeches (1952)
Stemming the Tide: Speeches 1951
   and 1952 (1953)
The Wisdom of Sir Winston
   Churchill (1956)
The Unwritten Alliance: Speeches
   1953 and 1959 (1961)
Winston S. Churchill: His Complete
   Speeches (1974)

Gathering storm
Opposition to appeasement

Following the defeat of the Conservatives in the 1929 General Election, Churchill entered into a period of political decline. When Prime Minister Ramsey Macdonald formed a coalition government in 1931, Churchill wasn't offered a Cabinet post – instead, he found himself relegated to the backbenches of the Conservative Party.

At this time Churchill increasingly found himself at odds with the government on a range of high profile political issues. His vehement opposition to Home Rule in India, which had wide cross-party support, made him unpopular with the Conservative hierarchy – not least because Churchill often used his connections with the British press to voice his dissent in essays and articles. Then the constitutional crisis surrounding the abdication of King Edward VIII in 1936 also damaged Churchill's reputation – he was seen to be actively supporting the king

Adolf Hitler

in contrast to the wishes of Parliament and the nation as a whole.

When Germany sent military forces into the Rhineland in February 1936, an action outlawed by the Treaty of Versailles, Prime Minister Stanley Baldwin's government decided against economic sanctions or military action. Acting on information he had received from his contacts in the military and civil service, Churchill had already warned of the dangers of German rearmament, proposing that Britain strengthened the Royal Air Force and created a Ministry of Defence. But public and political opinion was firmly opposed to any action that might have led to war, with many viewing Churchill's stance as overly hawkish and scaremongering.

On 12 November 1936, Churchill gave a rousing speech to the House of Commons, where he openly criticized the growing policy of appeasement that the government were following under the leadership of Prime Minister Neville Chamberlain:

The Government simply cannot make up their mind, or they cannot get the Prime Minister to make up his mind. So they go on in strange paradox, decided only to be undecided, resolved to be irresolute, adamant for drift, solid for fluidity, all powerful to be impotent. So we go on preparing more months and years—precious, perhaps vital to the greatness of Britain—for the locusts to eat.

When Hitler executed his long-held plan to annex Austria, which he outlined in his book *Mein Kampf* in early 1938, the response from the UK, France and the USA was again muted – despite the fact that Hitler's actions contravened the Treaty of Versailles. In Parliament, Chamberlain conceded to the House of Commons that 'The hard fact is that nothing could have arrested what has actually happened [in Austria] unless this country and other countries had been prepared to use force.'

Hitler became encouraged by the apathy and reticence of other European nations to coordinate action against Germany, so then he turned his attention to the Sudetenland, an area of Bohemia that had become a part of Czechoslovakia. When parts of the Austrian-Hungarian Empire were broken up after World War I, the nation of Czechoslovakia was formed under the Treaty of Versailles. The area known as the Sudetenland contained a large minority of ethnic German speakers, located especially close to the German border.

On 12 September 1938, Hitler encouraged Konrad Heinlein, the leader of the Sudeten Nazis, to rebel and instigate an uprising to demand union with Germany. The attempted putsch was quickly suppressed by the Czech army, causing Heinlein to flee to Germany. Continued violent unrest in the area, largely choreographed by Heinlein and the Nazis in Berlin, eventually caused the Czech government to impose martial law in the area. Hitler, an avowed supporter of the ethnic Germans in the Sudetenland, threatened to invade Czechoslovakia unless the Czech authorities ceded to the rebels' demands.

Chamberlain was now forced into action. He sent Lord Walter Runciman (see Quaffing Becherovka) as a special envoy of the British Government to attempt to broker a deal between the Czech government and the German rebels over the Sudetenland. However Runciman's mission failed, and he was recalled to London in the late summer.

On 15 September, Chamberlain himself flew to Germany and met with Hitler at Berchtesgaden. At this meeting, Hitler remained implacable in his demands that the Sudetenland should be absorbed into Germany or there would be war. Chamberlain, eager to avoid any conflict but without consultation with the Czech authorities, agreed for Germany to absorb areas near to the German border with a German population of more than 50 per cent. However Hitler then demanded that all the Sudetenland be given to Germany regardless of the ethnic composition of the different areas.

On 30 September, the infamous Munich Conference took place in which Chamberlain and Prime Minister Édouard Daladier of France, Mussolini and Hitler agreed to the Sudetenlands being handed over to Germany and for any disputed areas to be put before an international commission. As part of the negotiations, Chamberlain demanded that Hitler sign a peace treaty between Britain and Germany, thereby securing 'peace for our time'.

Churchill was fiercely opposed to any acquiescing to Hitler's demands. In letters to former Prime Minister David Lloyd George on the eve of the Munich Conference, he predicted that the negotiations gave only two alternatives for Britain, 'war or shame', with war highly likely to happen regardless. Churchill's prediction proved correct, as in March 1939 Hitler reneged on the Munich Agreement, invading the rest of Czechoslovakia before turning his attention to Poland, Britain and France. The attempts at appeasement had clearly failed, so Britain was left with no option but to decare war on Germany.

History, and particularly Churchill's own version in his book *The Gathering Storm* (1948) that details the events leading up to World War II, portrays Churchill's opposition to appeasement as a lone voice of dissent. Yet it is worth considering the political climate in which such appeasement policies were undertaken. Britain had endured a torrid decade of economic, social and political upheaval throughout the 1930s, so there was little appetite for entering into a potentially catastrophic global conflict if this could be avoided. Moreover, it should be understood that Churchill's primary concern was to strengthen Britain's defences in order to discourage any future hostilities – not, as it is often mistakenly believed, to challenge German expansion from the start.

Over time, the policy of appeasement has become part of British political folklore, and it has been used by subsequent Prime Ministers such as Margaret Thatcher and Tony Blair to justify military action in the Falklands War (1982) and invasion of Iraq (2003). However dubious the respective claims might be, it nevertheless seems that Churchill struck a chord that Britain would never be bullied again.

QUAFFING BECHEROVKA

One of the main criticisms of Lord Walter Runciman's failed mission to broker a deal during the Sudetenland crisis in 1938 (see Gathering Storm) concerned how the lord spent his leisure time in Czechoslovakia. Runciman and his team were accompanied on the trip by an eager press corps, and reports emerged afterwards that rather than being locked in tense and fraught negotiations, Runciman spent a good deal of his time partying with prominent members of the Nazi affiliated Sudeten German Party (SdP). While in Czechoslovakia, Runciman also spent time as a guest of Stephanie Julianne von Hohenlohe, an Austrian princess suspected of being a Nazi spy.

According to the historian Maria Dowling in her book **Czechoslovakia,** *Runciman was heartily wined and dined in the company of prominent local aristocratic Germans, who introduced him to the famous*

Becherovka

Czech drink named becherovka. This fearsomely strong herbal liqueur was originally developed as a cure for indigestion by an English physician to the court of the astonishingly-named Count Maximillian Freidrich von Plettenberg-Wittem-Mietingen.

Runciman appears to have been quite taken with the drink – at his behest, one of the summit meetings took place in the cellar of the becherovka factory in Carlsbad. On his return to Britain, Runicman set about importing the drink to be sold in various gentleman's clubs he frequented around London. Perhaps if Lord Runciman had spent more time getting to the bottom of the crisis, and less time quaffing becherovka, the situation wouldn't have escalated into one of the main catalysts for World War II.

'Winston is Back'
Returning from political exile

At 11am on 3 September 1939, Prime Minister Neville Chamberlain announced to the nation via a BBC radio broadcast that Britain had declared war on Germany. Chamberlain's speech clearly and concisely explained how diplomatic efforts to avoid war had failed, and that conflict was now inevitable:

We have a clear conscience. We have done all that any country could do to establish peace. But the situation in which no word given by Germany's ruler could be trusted, and no people or country could feel itself safe, had become intolerable. And now that we have resolved to finish it, I

know that you will all play your part with calmness and courage.

Although often portrayed as a ditherer and a reticent decision-maker, Chamberlain lost no time in reshuffling his government and creating a War Cabinet. The same day as war was declared, he summoned colleagues to Downing

Neville Chamberlain

Street to inform them of their role within an elite inner circle. Chamberlain's initial War Cabinet consisted of eight posts, alongside himself as Prime Minister, as follows:

Neville Chamberlain –
    Prime Minister and Leader of the House of Commons
Sir Samuel Hoare –
    Lord Privy Seal
Sir John Simon –
    Chancellor of the Exchequer
Lord Halifax – Secretary of State for Foreign Affairs
Leslie Hore-Belisha –
    Secretary of State for War
Sir Kingsley Wood –
    Secretary of State for Air
Winston Churchill –
    First Lord of the Admiralty
Lord Chatfield – Minister for Coordination of Defence
Lord Hankey –
    Minister without Portfolio

Most members of Chamberlain's War Cabinet were sitting ministers in his administration, with a few tweaks and swapping of positions. But the most sensational

and perhaps eyebrow-raising appointment was surely the return of Churchill to the post of First Lord of the Admiralty, a role he had undertaken during World War I until his tenure had ended in controversy (see War Strategist).

It is unclear exactly why Chamberlain chose to bring Churchill back from the 'wilderness', especially as Churchill had been a vociferous critic of Chamberlain's appeasement policies (see Gathering Storm). However it was a bold, if in the eyes of some members of the Conservative establishment at least, high-risk appointment, made by a politician whose name has become synonymous with political restraint.

It is probable that although Chamberlain and Churchill had found themselves at odds over the threat posed by Hitler and other high-profile political issues, Chamberlain nevertheless respected Churchill's military knowledge and experience. Legend has it that on hearing of Churchill's appointment, the Board of the Admiralty telegraphed every British naval ship and base with the message 'Winston is Back'.

Churchill immediately settled into his new role, returning to his old office at Admiralty House on the day following his appointment. To his astonishment, he found there the very same collection of sea maps he had used during his first spell at the Admiralty, almost a quarter of a century previously.

BEING PEDANTIC

On one occasion during World War II, after his appointment as Prime Minister, Churchill was preparing a speech to be broadcast to the nation. Having worked and reworked his draft many times, he finally sent the speech to be proofread by some of the clerks working in the Cabinet War Rooms.

Churchill was a perfectionist when it came to ensuring that his speeches were as clear as possible of any ambiguity or errors. However on this occasion the speech came back with a sentence rearranged and reworded; a note in the margin qualified the correction, explaining that it was 'bad grammar' to end a sentence with a preposition. According to legend, Churchill was furious at this criticism of his use of the English language. He allegedly distributed an angry memo around the war office that stated rather testily: 'This is the kind of arrant pedantry up with which I will not put.'

Although this story has entered into Churchill folklore and has been reported in various newspapers over the years – even appearing in books about English grammar – neither the corrected draft nor the Prime Minister's angry memo have survived in the Churchill archives and personal papers. However Churchill was right to question such 'pedantry'. While ending sentences with prepositions can scramble meaning and sound awkward, there are plenty of exceptions to this 'sacred cow' of grammar where it is perfectly acceptable to do so, particularly for rhetorical effect.

False start
Operation Wilfred put on hold

When Chuchill was re-appointed as First Lord of the Admiralty by Prime Minister Neville Chamberlain in September 1939 at the onset of World War II (see 'Winston is Back'), his first act was to draw up plans for a sea blockade in the North Sea to hinder Germany's ability to import valuable resources from Scandinavia. Germany had become heavily reliant on imported iron-ore reserves from Sweden, which it required to produce steel for its armaments and war machines. Churchill identified two principle routes used for the delivery of the Swedish iron ore, but the majority was transported via the Norwegian port of Narvik, which was free from floating ice-packs throughout the year. After being loaded at Narvik, the ore was then shipped on to Germany down the waterways that ran along the west coast of Norway.

The main issue for the British to overcome was that the route south from Narvik ran through the Indreled or Inner Leads, territorial

Damaged ship in the port of Narvik after Operation Wilfred

waters that belonged to Norway. As a neutral country in the conflict at that time, any attempt by the British navy to disrupt the passage of German ships would be seen as a violation of this neutrality in contravention of International Law. So Churchill came up with the solution of laying a minefield along the Indreled: this would force merchant ships out from Norwegian neutral waters into international ones, where the Royal Navy could sink or commandeer any carrying resources to Germany. In December 1939, Churchill issued a memorandum to the War Cabinet that outlined this proposal, which was codenamed Operation Wilfred.

The first seven months of World War II are sometimes referred to as the 'phoney war', owing to the relative inactivity of both sides in the conflict. Yet Churchill, mindful of the strategic importance of Scandinavia, pressed for the Cabinet to take decisive action on exports to Germany regardless of Norwegian neutrality. Thus on 6 January 1940, Secretary of State for Foreign Affairs Lord Halifax summoned the

Norwegian ambassador in London to inform him that the plan to mine the Indreled was going ahead. Predictably, both Norway and Sweden issued strong protests against the plan, temporarily forcing the initiative to be put on hold.

Operation Wilfred became further complicated by the so-called Winter War – the Soviet invasion of Finland in November 1939. Mindful that Soviet expansion in Scandinavia needed to be thwarted, given that Russia was allied to Germany at that point, Britain and France pledged support for Finland. However, this would not be possible without the support of Sweden and Norway, as they would need to transport troops and equipment through both countries. Churchill recognized an opportunity to use collective support for Finland to gain control of the routes used to transport the iron ore. He duly lobbied, and permission was granted in late February for the Admiralty to prepare the operation. However, a subsequent joint statement by Sweden, Norway and Denmark that French and British troops would be denied permission to use their lands as a gateway to Finland, along with the weakening of Finnish resistance to the Soviet Army, caused the plan to be abandoned.

Ultimately irrelevant
Operation Wilfred goes ahead

After Operation Wilfred was abandoned in the face of Scandinavian objections (see False Start), it then became linked to another of Churchill's proposals codenamed Operation Royal Marine, which planned to mine the Rhine on the Franco-German border. The French were reticent about Churchill's sister plan, as they feared it would antagonize the Germans into retaliatory measures – subsequently Operation Royal Marine was dropped. Yet on 3 April 1940 the War Cabinet finally gave permission for Operation Wilfred to go ahead – the Royal Navy were to lay the proposed minefields inside Norwegian waters.

The plan for Operation Wilfred called for three separate flotillas of ships, codenamed Force WS, Force WB and Force WV, to act in unison at separate strategic points along the Indreled. Force WS was to be the most southerly of the action forces and consisted of HMS *Teviot Bank,* a merchant ship requisitioned and converted into a minelayer, with four destroyers for protection; this flotilla was to lay mines on the waters of the Stadtlandet, the most westerly area of the Norwegian mainland. Force WB, consisting of two destroyers, was deployed as a decoy, to provide back-up, and also to disguise minelaying close to the fishing village of Bud. Force WV, the largest flotilla, was comprised of four minelaying destroyers and four destroyer escorts; it was detailed to lay mines in the Vestfjord, the waterway entrance into the port of Narvik.

Meanwhile the battle cruiser HMS *Renown,* under the command of Vice-Admiral W. J. Whitworth, was deployed to protect the minelayers, in case the Norwegians decided to employ their sea defences against a deliberate intrusion into their neutral waters. In the event, Churchill's plan was executed successfully. However, one of the protecting destroyers, HMS *Glowworm,* became detached from the convoy during the operation to search for a man who had fallen overboard.

On the morning of 8 April, HMS *Glowworm* came under fire from two German destroyers and engaged in battle. During the course of the engagement, the German battle cruiser *Admiral Hipper* inflicted fatal damage to HMS *Glowworm.* With his ship disabled and almost certainly doomed, Lieutenant Commander Gerard Broadmead-Roope gave the order for the *Glowworm* to ram the *Admiral Hipper.* This caused the bow to break off the *Glowworm* and the ship to sink, with the loss of 110 lives. Later Lieutenant Roope, who perished with his ship, was posthumously awarded the Victoria Cross, thus

becoming the first person in World War II to receive this honour.

Despite all of the dithering and diplomatic issues regarding Operation Wilfred, and its immediate success, ultimately Churchill's plan was proved to be completely irrelevant. Mindful of the Allied plans, Germany invaded Norway the following day – also with success. Now occupied by the Germans, the Norwegians found themselves under duress to align with their conquerors. In essence, Norway immediately lost her neutral status, so the waters around the country were no longer protected – they became fair game for the Allied navy.

Although some historians suggest that the Nazi invasion of Norway was a direct tit-for-tat response to Operation Wilfred, documents have revealed that the Germans, either

Admiral Hipper

through their own intelligence or intuition, were already aware of Churchill's plan and had put together their own operation. Germany had more or less decided to invade Norway as early as January 1940, but her leaders put the offensive off until the spring while the German army was still engaged in fighting the Polish resistance. Hitler ratified the memorandum that authorized the invasion on 7 March and the first German troop carriers set sail on 3 April, the same day that the British flotillas were assembled for Operation Wilfred. Indeed, Churchill gave an update on the Norwegian situation to Parliament on 11 April in which he refuted Germany's claim of retaliation for Operation Wilfred:

> The Nazi Government…have sought to make out that their invasion of Norway and of Denmark was a consequence of our action in closing the Norwegian corridor. It can, however, undoubtedly be proved that not only had their

preparations been made nearly a month before, but that their actual movements of troops and ships had begun before the British and French minefields were laid. No doubt they suspected they were going to be laid. It must indeed have appeared incomprehensible to them that they had not been laid long before. They therefore decided in the last week of March to use the Norwegian corridor to send empty ore ships northward, filled with military stores and German soldiers, concealed below decks, in order at the given moment to seize the various ports on the Norwegian seaboard which they considered to have military value.

WILFRED THE RABBIT

The name of Operation Wilfred (see False Start and Ultimately Irrelevant) was chosen by Churchill, and refers to a long-running strip cartoon in the Daily Mirror newspaper that was popular at the time. The eponymous characters were, in turn, a dog named Pip, a penguin named Squeak, and a lop-eared rabbit named Wilfred. Churchill, a fan of the strip, chose the name of Wilfred for his Norwegian stealth campaign as he believed it to be a small, but potentially decisive, strategic maneuver.

However Doris Lessing's assertion in her autobiography of 2007 is a small irony — if it is indeed true. Here she suggests that the character of Wilfred the rabbit was based in part upon the Russian revolutionary Leon Trotsky. Had he known, this would have appalled Churchill, given his high-profile disgust for the Russian Revolution and Bolshevism.

'Walking with destiny'
Entering Number 10 as Prime Minister

On 7 May 1940, the House of Commons began sitting at around 2.45pm to debate what was termed 'the conduct of the war', but is known historically as the Norway Debate. Few members on their way to Parliament that day could have anticipated that they were about to be involved in such a momentous Parliamentary debate.

Prime Minister Neville Chamberlain began the debate by attempting to absolve himself and his War Cabinet from any direct blame for the failure of the Norwegian Campaign. Indeed, he even tried to suggest that although the Allied forces had been forced to retreat, their losses were minimal in comparison to the German ones. The Labour Opposition took great exception to Chamberlain's attempts to 'spin' the Allied defeat, supported by influential backbench Conservatives.

The debate continued in Parliament the following day, with

the Labour Opposition calling for a vote of confidence in the government. To the surprise of many members, Chamberlain accepted the challenge, stating: 'No Government can prosecute a war efficiently unless it has public and Parliamentary support'. He also defiantly goaded detractors from his own party with the words: 'at least we shall see who is with us and who is against us'.

The debate continued throughout the day, with Chamberlain and his Cabinet receiving withering criticism from all sides of the House of Commons, most notably from the former Prime Minister, David Lloyd George. Meanwhile Churchill spoke in defence of Chamberlain, and in his role as First Lord of the Admiralty, at one point offered to take full responsibility for any errors of judgement in the Norwegian Campaign.

However, it transpired that larger issues concerned Lloyd George, such as Chamberlain's failed appeasement policy and the failure to properly fund and re-arm British forces during the 1930s – the opposition parties started to smell blood. In the event, the government survived the vote of confidence by 81 votes. But given that the Conservative Party held a huge majority in the House of Commons, it became clear that over a hundred Tory MPs had either voted with the opposition or had deliberately abstained.

10 Downing Street

The following day, Chamberlain attempted to reunite a broken and divided Parliament by forming a new cross-party coalition along the lines of the government led by Lloyd George during World War I. Clement Attlee, Leader of the Opposition Labour Party, while not averse to joining a Conservative-led coalition, categorically stated that his party would not serve under any administration led by Chamberlain. The position taken by Attlee and Labour effectively left Chamberlain with no option but to resign as Prime Minister.

A meeting was hurriedly convened between Chamberlain, Churchill, Lord Halifax and David Margesson, the government Chief Whip. The accepted version of events is that Lord Halifax was Chamberlain's preferred choice to succeed him, but that Halifax himself had reservations on the grounds that he sat in the House of Lords and not in the Commons. It is also likely that the Labour Party would have regarded the appointment of Lord Halifax as the 'establishment' choice, and may therefore have refused to join the coalition. This left Churchill as the only alternative.

Thus on 10 May 1940, as tradition decreed, King George VI summoned Winston Churchill to Buckingham Palace to formally ask him to become Prime Minister. It was the culmination of a career in politics that had spanned four decades, and the realization of Churchill's life-long ambition. In his collection of memoirs entitled *The Second World War* (1948–1953), Churchill described his feelings on entering 10 Downing Street as Prime Minister for the first time as 'walking with destiny'. After years in the political wilderness, Churchill had finally been offered the highest office and a chance to prove himself worthy. This was an opportunity that he was determined not to waste, as the stakes were much greater than his own professional self-fulfilment.

BARBED NOTE

There is an apocryphal story that the great Anglo-Irish playwright George Bernard Shaw (1856–1950) once wrote to Churchill to invite him to attend the premier of a new work. Shaw enclosed two tickets, with a barbed note attached that invited Churchill to 'bring a friend' – if he, indeed, had any. Churchill is said to have replied that he couldn't make the first night of the new production, but would attend the second 'if there is one'.

George Bernard Shaw

Triumph of sorts
Evaluating Operation Dynamo

Operation Dynamo was the codename given to the massive operation to evacuate the British Expeditionary Force (BEF) and other Allied forces from France after Germany invaded the country in May 1940. It has given rise to the notion of the 'Dunkirk spirit', an indomitable attitude to stand firm against seemingly overwhelming odds – but was the operation really a success? In truth it should, and could, have been seen as a humiliation for Britain: at the time, Hitler believed that his forces had over-powered the Allies and won a famous victory. However the mere scale and ad-hoc nature of the planning of Operation Dynamo have cemented its place in history as a key moment of World War II.

Churchill had initially believed that if luck was on their side, 40,000 to 50,000 troops of the BEF could be evacuated from Dunkirk. In the event, almost 340,000 troops were saved over the nine days of the operation. No doubt a mixture of good fortune and some uncharacteristic dithering by the German High Command played their part in this achievement. Nevertheless, the sheer bloody-mindedness of a rescue force made up of merchant ships, fishing boats and hearty volunteers in privately-owned vessels, backed up by the Royal Navy, somehow managed to turn what appeared from the outset to be a hopeless situation into a triumph of sorts.

In an address to Parliament on 4 June 1940, Churchill described the Dunkirk evacuation as 'A miracle of deliverance', although he qualified any accusations of hyperbole by noting that 'We must be very careful not to assign to this deliverance the attributes of a victory. Wars are not won by evacuations.'

However perhaps the most telling impact of Dunkirk, alongside that of Britain retaining valuable manpower and resources to help

Troops evacuated from Dunkirk

continue the fight against Hitler, was that Operation Dynamo was widely reported in the USA and helped to bring about a groundswell of support for sending assistance to the Allies in Europe. Indeed, an impassioned and dramatic editorial appeared in the *New York Times* on 1 June 1940, halfway through Operation Dynamo, which revealed that American public opinion was rapidly moving towards intervention. Praising the courage of the Allies, it described how the Dunkirk evacuation had exposed the 'soul of democracy', and would continue to be honoured in the English language for ever.

BLOOD AND SWEAT

Churchill's appointment to the position of Prime Minister in May 1940 (see 'Walking with Destiny') was viewed with scepticism by many of his political contemporaries, not least within his own party. However, Churchill proved to be a popular choice with the public at large, and was met by cheering crowds outside 10 Downing Street after he had accepted the post.

On 14 May the London Evening Standard published a now famous cartoon to commemorate the appointment. This depicted a determined and bullish-looking Churchill striding purposefully forwards, rolling up his shirtsleeves as if preparing for a brawl, with an army of politicians following in his wake. The caption underneath contained the now immortal line: 'All behind you, Winston'.

But on the day that Churchill was appointed Prime Minister, Germany invaded the Low Countries of Belgium and the Netherlands, and were pushing on towards France – World War II had now truly begun. Therefore on 13 May, which was Whit Monday and should have been a national holiday, Churchill convened a special sitting of Parliament, delivering his first speech as Prime Minister.

In this speech, Churchill summoned all his powers of oratory, as he asked for the House to vote in support of his newly created coalition. After announcing the reconstruction of the government, Churchill went on to state: 'we are in the preliminary stage of one of the greatest battles in history' and that much preparation needed to be done.

This speech, commonly referred to as Churchill's 'Blood, Toil, Tears and Sweat' speech, is one of his most famous, and helped to galvanize support from all sides of the House of Commons for his plans – as it turned out, Churchill's motion to support the coalition was unanimously passed by the House. Below are some excerpts for the speech:

I would say to the House, as I said to those who have joined this Government: 'I have nothing to offer but blood, toil, tears and sweat.' We have before us an ordeal of the most grievous kind. We have before us many, many long months of struggle and of suffering.

You ask, what is our aim? I can answer in one word: It is victory, victory at all costs, victory in spite of all terror, victory, however long and hard the road may be; for without victory, there is no survival.

I feel sure that our cause will not be suffered to fail among men. At this time I feel entitled to claim the aid of all, and I say, 'Come then, let us go forward together with our united strength.'

Oratory skills
Galvanizing a nation

Churchill was renowned in parliamentary circles for his oratory skills, although some found his style often a little too verbose, and his use of quaint or old-fashioned vocabulary deliberately obstructive. However, once ensconced at 10 Downing Street, Churchill recognized the need to make powerful statements that would galvanize the nation for the war effort. As the war escalated, dramatic events across the English Channel provided the perfect backdrop for Churchill, a highly skilled writer, to bring all of his skills as an orator to the fore.

Churchill's three most famous speeches during the war were all made within a few weeks of him taking over as Prime Minister: his opening salvo to request the support of his hastily formed coalition on 13 May 1940 (see Blood and Sweat); the speech known as 'We Shall Fight on the Beaches', which was delivered to the House of Commons on 4 June 1940; and 'Their Finest Hour' speech, which was delivered to the House of Commons on 18 June 1940 then broadcast to the nation on the same evening.

In contrast to most modern politicians, Churchill didn't employ speechwriters or advisers – as a multiple published author and former journalist, he had full confidence in his own copy. Nonetheless, Churchill took great care and attention over his speeches,

House of Commons

drafting and redrafting them several times over to make minor adjustments and amendments. Moreover, embarrassed and ridiculed in his youth for his speech impediment (see Distinctive Diction), Churchill came to regard this as a signature of sorts, which he felt added authenticity to his words. While preparing his speeches, he would read them aloud to measure the precise cadence and rhythm of the words.

In many senses, Churchill's most memorable speeches took on classical forms of oratory. In his memoirs, Churchill writes of trying to compose his speeches using a modified psalm form: in classical psalms, the speaker sets out a problem that needs to be addressed, and in summary provides a message of hope. Churchill's combined use of emotive language, cleverly chosen dramatic metaphors, and powerful imagery were other key signposts in his speeches.

'We shall fight on the beaches'
In perhaps his most famous 'We Shall Fight on the Beaches'

speech, Churchill skilfully deploys a rhetorical device known as anaphora. Thus the summary of the speech appears to contain a defiant rallying cry, which has become culturally synonymous with a never-say-die attitude:

> We shall go on to the end. We shall fight in France, we shall fight on the seas and oceans, we shall fight with growing confidence and growing strength in the air, we shall defend our island, whatever the cost may be. We shall fight on the beaches, we shall fight on the landing grounds, we shall fight in the fields and in the streets, we shall fight in the hills; we shall never surrender…

Churchill's use of anaphora is in the deliberate repetition of the phrase 'we shall fight'. Churchill knew that this would create a strong sense of unity and common purpose for the dark and torrid times ahead. Yet Churchill was actually saying: since France is about to fall, there is a real chance that Britain will be invaded next; he is therefore trying to provide a rallying call to say that although Britain is quite likely to lose, she will never give up.

Another interesting aspect of the much-quoted 'We Shall Fight' speech is the belief that it was broadcast to the nation over the radio, with a voice actor named Norman Shelley voicing the words. In fact, the often-played recording was made several years after the war by Churchill himself, who was encouraged to do so for the sake of posterity. The speech was only ever delivered to the House of Commons on 4 June 1940, with excerpts read out in news bulletins and reprinted in the press.

The final few lines of the speech are also worthy of consideration. When a speech is quoted as a motivational spur, it is common to finish with the line 'we shall never surrender'. However Churchill goes on to speculate what may happen if Britain was to be invaded by German forces:

Churchill recorded his 'We Shall Fight' speech after the war

...and even if, which I do not for a moment believe, this island or a large part of it were subjugated and starving, then our Empire beyond the seas, armed and guarded by the British Fleet, would carry on the struggle, until, in God's good time, the new world, with all its power and might, steps forth to the rescue and the liberation of the old.

Although the USA was still officially neutral at this point, Churchill had been lobbying for American support in the fight against Hitler. President Franklin D. Roosevelt had asked for reassurances from Churchill that should Britain fall the British government would refuse to capitulate its navy, but detach it instead to the colonies. In theory, this would then leave the way clear for the USA to enter the conflict in Europe.

'Their finest hour'

Following the fall of Paris two weeks later, Churchill again addressed the House of Commons on 18 June 1940 in a speech that is also revered for its dramatic peroration and climax. The main body of Churchill's 'Their Finest Hour' speech is in the form of a report that details the success of the recent evacuation of Dunkirk and anticipates the forthcoming Battle of Britain.

At one point, while reiterating the need for 'every man and every woman' to 'have the chance to show the finest qualities of their race', Churchill slips in a quotation from Andrew Marvell's poem *An Horatian Ode on Cromwell's Return*

from Ireland (1650):

> He nothing common did
>   or mean,
> Upon that memorable scene.

Churchill uses the Andrew Marvell quotation to reinforce his core message that the country must steel itself to fight to the death for a just cause.

Churchill concludes his speech by praising France and the courage of the French in the face of the enemy, and by pledging British solidarity with the French in the struggle to restore their freedom and the freedom of Europe from tyranny.

Andrew Marvell

Churchill's closing remarks still retain the power to send a shiver down the spine over 75 years later:

I expect that the battle of Britain is about to begin. Upon this battle depends the survival of Christian civilisation. Upon it depends our own British life and the long continuity of our institutions and our Empire. The whole fury and might of the enemy must very soon be turned on us. Hitler knows that he will have to break us in this island or lose the war. If we can stand up to him all Europe may be free, and the life of the world may move forward into broad, sunlit uplands; but if we fail then the whole world, including the United States, and all that we have known and cared for, will sink into the abyss of a new dark age made more sinister, and perhaps more prolonged, by the lights of a perverted science. Let us therefore brace ourselves to our duty and so bear ourselves that if the British Commonwealth and Empire lasts for a thousand years men will still say, 'This was their finest hour.'

DRUNK DURING ADDRESS?

The radio transmission of the 'Their Finest Hour' speech (see Oratory Skills) has gone down in British political folklore – yet it wasn't quite so enthusiastically received at the time. Some of Churchill's parliamentary colleagues felt that the broadcast lacked the power and intensity of his original address to Parliament – although this may be because speaking into a microphone in a radio studio is vastly different to speaking on the floor of the House of Commons.

Moreover Cecil King, the owner of the **Daily Mirror** *newspaper group and a staunch critic of Churchill, slyly suggested that some sections of the broadcast were slurred on account of Churchill being drunk. However Churchill is thought to have recorded the broadcast while smoking one of his beloved cigars, and this, allied* *to his natural lisp, contributed to this impression. Nonetheless, the broadcast proved popular with the general public, as a Home Office opinion poll at the time returned Churchill with an almost 90 per cent approval rating.*

Nerve centre
Role of the Cabinet War Rooms

The plan to create a central office of operations in Britain from which to conduct any future conflicts was first mooted by military and defence staff in the 1920s. At the time, intelligence on Germany's stockpiling of armaments led military strategists to predict large-scale devastation and civilian losses from any sustained bombing campaign against London.

So in the first instance emergency evacuation plans were drawn up to ensure the safety of the Prime Minister and his Cabinet along with high-ranking military personnel. However concerns were raised that if the government was perceived to be abandoning the capital, this might have a detrimental effect upon the morale of the general public. If London was vulnerable to surprise attack, there were also concerns about how such an evacuation policy could be implemented at short notice.

A solution was therefore devised to build an emergency bunker to protect members of the British High Command. Germany's military manoeuvres to annex Austria in March 1938 (see Gathering Storm) brought matters to a head, and a site was chosen to build the command shelter. The Cabinet War Rooms were to be housed in the New Public Offices building, a Whitehall storage space used to house government archives.

This choice of location was determined by its proximity to Downing Street and the Houses of Parliament, and the belief that the building's steel structure would be able to withstand a bomb attack. A large protective concrete slab was laid above the bunker to add extra protection, although military experts have since conceded that a direct hit on the Cabinet

War Rooms would have been devastating – initial estimations that the building was 'bomb-proof' were, in fact, wishful thinking.

In May 1938 work began on hurriedly converting the building to make it fit for purpose. Rooms were cleared and partitions were erected, and telecommunications lines, a new ventilation system, and an ingenious air-lock defence system to guard against possible gas attacks were installed. The layout of the building was centred around the Map Room, which was very much the nerve centre of military operations, as well as the central information and intelligence hub.

Although the facility was theoretically available for use in late 1938, further modifications had to be carried out. Indeed, there was no provision for accommodation, or even toilet facilities, until

The London Blitz

midway through 1939. The Cabinet War Rooms were finally officially opened and became fully operational on 27 August 1939, just a week before Britain declared war on Germany.

During the early months of the war, the expected aerial bombardment didn't take place. In fact, the War Cabinet didn't actually meet in their new shelter until late October 1939 – even on that occasion they convened mainly to test out the facilities. Yet the Cabinet War Rooms really came into their own during the nine months of the Blitz between September 1940 and May 1941. During that period Churchill's War Cabinet held meetings there 115 times, although the Chiefs of Staff and the Defence Committee met in the location on a regular basis throughout the war.

Churchill and his wife, Clementine, had their own private bedrooms in the building, but as he had an aversion to sleeping underground it is thought that he only slept in the Cabinet War Rooms on a handful of occasions.

Remington Noiseless typewriter

Yet Churchill made regular use of his quarters for his afternoon 'power nap', part of his daily routine to recharge his batteries. The typists and administration staff were informed of Churchill's 'nap time' by a loud tapping on the ventilation pipes, which was the signal for them to keep as quiet as possible and not to disturb him. Then Churchill would tap again when he had finished his nap to inform staff that it was business as usual again.

When Churchill took over as Prime Minister he insisted that all of the administration staff in the Cabinet War Rooms use only a particular model of typewriter.

Made by the US company Remington, this had a patented Noiseless mechanism to cut down on the endless clacking from the typing pool. Churchill also designed and had printed a stock of red stationery labels for use in the Cabinet War Rooms – as he was not known to be the most patient of men, the labels contained the words 'ACTION THIS DAY' printed in bold black type.

Following the Blitz, the threat from Luftwaffe aerial assaults subsided so Churchill and his War Cabinet were able to meet at either 10 Downing Street or the Houses of Parliament. However, the Cabinet War Rooms remained in operation throughout the war for 24 hours a day, right up until the surrender of Japan on 14 August 1945. Two days later the lights were switched off in the Map Room.

Entrance to the Cabinet War Rooms

Although the value of preserving the Cabinet War Rooms was recognized early on, access to the public was first limited by appointment only, owing to security concerns surrounding the building's close proximity to other key government departments. But in 1981 Prime Minister Margaret Thatcher decided to widen public access to the site, and the Imperial War Museum agreed to restore the building and take over administration of the project.

Thatcher and the Imperial War Museum officially opened the Cabinet War Rooms as a museum in 1984. Then in 2005 a second museum holding a permanent exhibition on the life of Winston Churchill was installed inside. The now renamed Churchill War Rooms has become a popular attraction for tourists and visitors from all over the world. The mix of lived-in history and modern interactive displays has provided new generations with a clear insight into the workings of Churchill's war machine.

SECRET REPLICA

Churchill had a replica of his operational Cabinet War Rooms (see Nerve Centre) constructed at a secret location in London – he was concerned that the proximity of the Whitehall Cabinet War Rooms to key government buildings had created a prime target for bombers. The replica bunker was constructed 12m (40ft) beneath a building in Neasden, North London, and was encased in steel-reinforced concrete that measured almost 1m (4ft) thick.

Codenamed Paddock, the existence of this replica was top secret – even King George VI was unaware of its existence. In fact, Churchill even refused to reveal its whereabouts in his memoirs after

Corridor in Paddock

the war, vaguely writing that the Paddock was 'somewhere near Hampstead'. The site is now owned by a housing association, and can be visited by the public via appointment on certain days of the year.

Siren suit
Creating a 'onesie'

Despite nicknaming his all-in-one creation a siren suit, owing to its usefulness during air raids in World War II, Churchill had actually conceived the idea for this special leisure suit a decade earlier. His design was inspired by the overalls first sported by pilots and mechanics in the 1910s to protect their clothing, which he adapted for use as a comfortable item of clothing to be worn around his home.

When the Nazis started bombing Britain in 1940, Churchill found that his all-in-one was the perfect item of clothing to don in a hurry when the sirens sounded – it was roomy, warm, and easy to put on quickly over his night clothes. He therefore commissioned the outfitters Turnbull and Asser to make up more of the hooded garments, which each came with a belt, zipper, and large pockets.

In total, Churchill ordered 12 siren suits of various styles and fabrics from his outfitters. Between them, these were suitable for all occasions, and included a pinstripe version for formal wear, one in the style of an army dress uniform, and even a green velvet all-in-one that was designed specifically for Churchill to wear in the Cabinet War Rooms (see Nerve Centre).

So fond was he of his siren suits that Churchill wore them regularly, and was often photographed with famous dignitaries and heads of state while wearing, as he also called them, these 'romper' suits. Indeed, during Churchill's visit to the White House in 1941, his attire must have impressed First Lady Eleanor Roosevelt, as she later told reporters that she was going to have one made for the President!

Siren suits became very popular with the public during World War

11. They were practical during air raids, and they could be bought ready-made, usually made from wool – but for those with limited income or not enough clothing coupons, sewing patterns were available to make a 'do-it-yourself' version. In the era of rationing, ingenuity was often necessary, so it was not uncommon for items such as curtains to be turned into all-in-ones, or for a siren suit that a child had outgrown to be transformed into a pair of trousers.

In the 1950s, Churchill wore his all-in-one creations while he sat for the painter Frank O. Salisbury and the sculptor Oscar Nemon, after which he presented the siren suit in question to Nemon as a souvenir. Only three of the original one-pieces are now known to be in existence, including the green velvet version: one of these was sold in 2002 for the sum of £29,875; meanwhile another of the surviving siren suits is now on permanent display at the Churchill War Rooms (see Nerve Centre).

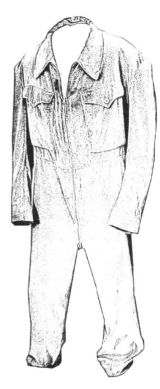

One of Churchill's siren suits

IN-JOKE

In one of the corridors of the Cabinet War Rooms (see Nerve Centre) is a small wooden changeable sign hanging on the wall. This was the War Rooms' weather board, which was there to inform the inhabitants, who spent many long hours underground, what the weather was like outside. As an in-joke, whenever an air raid was due or in progress the board was always changed to say 'WINDY'.

Despite the instalment of a reinforced concrete slab that measured up to 3m (10ft) thick above the rooms in December 1940, it is estimated that over half the bombs dropped on London would have been large enough to destroy the building with a direct hit. The Cabinet War Rooms were also in danger of flooding, as they were built well below the level of the River Thames.

Force of personality
Helping the Allies towards victory

It is commonly accepted that the intervention of the USA and Hitler's invasion of the Soviet Union were both key turning points in World War II. Nevertheless, Churchill's leadership contributed to the Allies' success in several key ways.

Streamlined the decision making process

As Churchill knew only too well, key decisions in military strategy need to be decisively made – success is all about timing, as well as a modicum of good luck. Churchill learned from the disaster at Gallipoli (see War Strategist) and the failure of his Norwegian Campaign (see Ultimately Irrelevant) that the dithering of politicians alongside any separation between the military and the mechanics of government could prove fatal to the best laid plans.

Thus, one of his first acts when taking over as Prime Minister in 1940 was to create a new post for himself as Minister of Defence, which effectively made Churchill the commander-in-chief of the armed forces. Keen to avoid the endless committee meetings redolent of Prime Minister Neville Chamberlain's handling of the early months of the war, Churchill re-shaped the War Cabinet, re-directing considerable resources into intelligence gathering networks.

Employed words as weapons

There is an apocryphal story that at the climax of Churchill's 'We Shall Fight on the Beaches' speech to Parliament (see Oratory Skills), he sat down and muttered to a colleague 'we shall fight them on the streets with broken bottles because that is basically all we have got'. Although the hurried evacuation of troops from France via Dunkirk preserved manpower, a large stock of military hardware and munitions were abandoned during the process. Naturally, it would take time to rebuild and restock in order to mount a successful resistance or counter attack against Germany.

Churchill therefore spent the next few months in his speeches to Parliament and the nation deploying his own personal armoury – the power of words. His oratory skills helped him bring hope to the British nation during the dark hours of the Blitz of 1940 and 1941. Meanwhile his message of defiance struck a profound chord with the British public at large, helping to galvanize them for the struggle ahead.

Forged and maintained delicate alliances

Before World War II, Churchill was hardly renowned for his skills as a diplomat. Having twice changed his political allegiances in Parliament, and being notorious for his stubborn streak, few people inside the political establishment would have backed him as a leader able to maintain delicate alliances with the Allied powers. However, Churchill was convinced that the defeat of Germany needed the vital support of the USA, so he went out of his way to court and curry favour with President Franklin D. Roosevelt in the lead up to the USA's entrance into the conflict in 1941.

Joseph Stalin

between Britain, the USA and the Soviet Union during the war years, uniting the three powers against a common enemy.

Took some radical decisions

One of Churchill's most controversial appointments to his War Cabinet was inviting his friend and confidant Lord Beaverbrook to become Minister of Aircraft Production. A media baron and a prominent businessman, William Maxwell Aitken, 1st Lord Beaverbook (1879–1964), had used his newspapers during the late 1930s to support the Chamberlain government in their policies of appeasement towards Germany. Yet when Churchill became Prime Minister in May 1940, he handed responsibility for reviewing and overhauling the aircraft production industries to Beaverbrook, appointing him Minister of Aircraft Production.

Similarly when Russia joined the Allies, it must have taken no small amount of discretion to forge and maintain a strong working relationship with Joseph Stalin. After all, Churchill had been a very outspoken opponent of the Russian Revolution two decades previously, loudly declaring that Bolshevism needed to be 'strangled at birth'. Although relations between Britain and the Soviet Union soured rapidly after World War II, Churchill nonetheless managed to sustain an awkward and often fraught alliance

This appointment was not popular with Churchill's newly formed and fledgling coalition, some believing it smacked of cronyism on his part – but

Beaverbrook's sharp business acumen proved more than up to the job. Under his guidance, within a year British aircraft production had increased dramatically by around 15 per cent – vital at that critical point in the war. And by streamlining the management and working practices of floundering production plants, by seizing control of Royal Air Force maintenance and supplies units, and by calling upon the knowledge and skills of interned German Jewish immigrant engineers and workers, aircraft production flourished under Beaverbrook's watch.

Churchill, no doubt delighted that his political gamble had paid dividends, championed Beaverbrook's war contribution. Likewise, an editorial on 16 September 1940 in the US publication *Time Magazine* also championed his contribution, claiming that Beaverbrook could not be held accountable if Britain fell in the autumn – but if she survived, this result could be considered as his 'triumph'.

There is some debate among historians over the influence on wartime production that Beaverbrook's industrial reforms actually had. For example, there is an argument that aircraft production and output had been steadily improving prior to his appointment, and that the impact of his initiatives has been somewhat over-stated. Nonetheless, the energy that Beaverbrook brought to the role, despite frequent arguments with the Air Ministry, helped to create a

Lord Beaverbrook

valuable hike in aircraft production – as did his fabled appeal for housewives to donate scrap metal, particularly aluminium pots and pans, for recycling in advance of the Battle of Britain (see Doing Their Bit).

Sheer hard work and force of personality

Ultimately, Churchill's greatest contribution to the war effort was his unwavering belief in the need to dig in and resist, even if it meant fighting to the very end. Allied to this was the extraordinary hard work and commitment he personally contributed to the cause. Regularly working 18 to 20 hours a day and surviving on very little sleep, Churchill pushed himself to the very limits of physical and mental endurance – in fact, to the point of near meltdown from exhaustion at several points. This was all the more astonishing and remarkable considering that Churchill was in his late 60s during the war.

DOING THEIR BIT

During World War II, Churchill appointed Lord Beaverbrook as Minister of Aircraft Production (see Force of Personality). So with Churchill's blessing, Beaverbrook launched a public appeal to the nation, and specifically housewives, to donate items of scrap metal, particularly anything made from aluminium, to aid the war effort. The Women's Volunteer Services hurriedly organized spaces to receive the donations around the country, with another thousand 'dumping centres' springing up across the land virtually overnight.

Beaverbrook's appeal was a roaring success in terms of participation – and it wasn't only pots and pans that were donated. Everything from bicycle mudguards and door handles to hair curlers and car registration plates were submitted. A collection point in Westminster even received a metal artificial leg, and another in Chelsea found a crushed motor racing car among the offerings.

However, it is highly unlikely that any of the collected metal was actually used in the creation of any aircraft – in the event, it was recycled and used for other purposes. Yet as a propaganda campaign, the donation of scrap metal helped to add to the growing sense across the British nation that everyone needed to pull together and do their bit for the war effort.

High honour
Becoming Lord Warden of the Cinque Ports

In September 1941, King George VI conferred on Winston Churchill the title of Lord Warden of the Cinque Ports, one of the highest honours that can be bestowed by a British monarch – and one that Churchill readily accepted. Since the time of King Henry VIII, the title has been honorary and awarded for life, the recipients usually being members of the royal family, or Prime Ministers who have played a significant role in defending Britain during times of war.

Prior to its honorary significance, from at least the 12th century onwards the incumbent of the position had held sole charge of the five significant port towns on the south-east coast of England: Dover, Hastings, Hythe, Romney and Sandwich. These five towns comprised the Cinque Ports of the title, and in return for certain privileges they supplied the sovereign with a navy. Today,

14 coastal towns make up the confederation of Cinque Ports – some of Churchill's famous predecessors to the title include William Pitt, Lord Palmerston and the Duke of Wellington.

Despite his appointment in 1941, Churchill's investiture ceremony at Dover Castle had to be deferred until 1946 due to the location's close proximity to German artillery across the Channel coupled with the risk of Luftwaffe raids. Together with the title came an impressive Lord Warden's uniform, which Churchill loved to sport and took the opportunity to wear at any ceremonial event – either connected to the office or not. He is depicted in portraits on at least

Churchill dressed for Queen Elizabeth's coronation in his Lord Warden's uniform

three occasions donning the regalia and he wore it to Queen Elizabeth II's coronation, reputedly saying that as Prime Minister he should not be outshone by anyone at the ceremony other than the queen herself. While back in residence at Chartwell at the conclusion of World War II, Churchill proudly flew the heraldic flags of the Lord Warden from the flagpole.

On Churchill's death in 1965, the title of Lord Warden of the Cinque Ports was endowed upon Sir Robert Menzies, the former Prime Minister of Australia, and subsequently Queen Elizabeth the Queen Mother in 1978. The current holder of the title is Admiral of the Fleet Baron Michael Boyce.

GOLD-PLATED

Winston Churchill was well aware that his voice was distinctive because of his famous speech impediment (see Distinctive Diction) – he therefore didn't want to do anything to change, in any way, the delivery of his famous speeches. Thus, when he required dentures in later life, it was important that they didn't vary his recognizable lisp. To ensure that this didn't happen, at around the start of World War II Churchill employed the services of the eminent dental surgeon William Fish to specifically design loose-fitting dentures that would enable him to retain his widely renowned style of oration. Fish's dental technician, Derek Cudlipp, subsequently constructed what is thought to have been four identical sets of the gold-plated teeth.

Churchill's gold-plated dentures

So highly did Churchill value Fish's work that he nominated him for a knighthood. Moreover, when Derek Cudlipp received his call-up papers, Churchill personally tore them up, maintaining that it was more important to the war effort that Cudlipp remain in London to be on hand if the Prime Minister's dentures needed repair. But while visiting the US President in 1942, one of Churchill's teeth became displaced and had to be repaired by Roosevelt's dentist instead. At around this time, dental practitioners in the USA generally held a low opinion of British dentistry – it therefore pleased Fish's team to discover that the repair was not up to their standard, with a cement border clearly visible.

In 2010 a partial set of Churchill's false teeth was sold at auction to a private collector for £15,200, three times the expected price. Meanwhile the second set is on display at the Hunterian Museum in London, labelled 'the teeth that saved the world'. It is believed that the third set was melted down, and that the fourth was buried with its famous owner.

Ignominious defeat
Outcome of the 1945 General Election

In the 1945 General Election, Clement Attlee and Labour defeated Winston Churchill and the Conservatives. At the time, this defeat was considered to be a major shock, not least because the margin of victory – a Labour Party majority of 145 seats – was the largest ever recorded in a British General Election. Churchill had

Clement Attlee

called the General Election for 5 July 1945, just two months after VE Day, no doubt believing that his personal popularity rating and public euphoria over the end of the war would carry him to a comfortable victory. In the event, the election proved to be a disaster for his party.

Political historians and commentators have long discussed the possible reasons behind Labour's landslide victory. While it is true that Churchill was still a hugely popular figure with the public at large, the party he represented was not. Unwittingly Churchill was also, perhaps, the architect of his own downfall. He had invited prominent members of the opposition Labour Party into his wartime coalition Cabinet, which had allowed the likes of Clement Attlee and Ernest Bevan to increase their profile in the public eye, and to demonstrate their competence and suitability to govern. Churchill had taken the decision in a time of crisis to ensure stability and strength in the government and Parliament during the war. However, although the Conservatives were the majority party in the coalition, the public did not see the war victory as a Conservative victory, but rather a collaborative coalition one.

Another key factor in the outcome of the election was the publication in 1942 of the Beveridge Report. This landmark survey outlined key areas for social reform in Britain and proved to be hugely popular with the public. Churchill reluctantly accepted some of the recommendations, but insisted that their implementation should not detract from the war effort – any meaningful programme of reform should be put to the public at a General Election afterwards. This delay tactic proved fateful, as the Labour Party outside the government actively campaigned for the reform agenda, garnering widespread popular support. It is arguable that even if Churchill had provided an alternative programme for post-war reform, his popularity could have carried him to victory. Yet his reticence to do so had a detrimental effect on his party.

In the later years of World War II, left-wing newspapers mounted a sustained attack on the Conservatives, centred largely on the party's pre-war record in government. They apportioned blame for the war on the failure of appeasement policies, economic mismanagement, and the failure to rearm. Churchill and his advisers may have thought, perhaps complacently, that the jubilation engendered by victory over the Nazis would cause the people of Britain to forgive and forget. But newspapers such as the *Daily Mirror* – run by Cecil King, a long-time nemesis of Churchill's – made sure that they didn't.

In the end, after a long, brutal and destructive period of war, the appetite for change in Britain was very strong. This meant that the Conservatives, seen as the party of the establishment and the bastions of the old order, were not viewed as the party to usher in the reforms and rebuild the social and economic fabric of the country – regardless of their heroic and charismatic leader, Winston Churchill.

As it turned out, Churchill retained the leadership of the Conservative Party, continuing as a high profile and outspoken force in his new position as Leader of the Opposition. Churchill led his party at the 1950 General Election, clawing back a large number of seats in Parliament and leaving Labour's previous majority in tatters. In the 1951 General Election, just 12 months later, he returned the Conservatives to government. This rebuilding of the Conservative popular vote during his six years as Leader of the Opposition was a considerable political achievement. However, it is his spectacular defeat at the end of World War II that history recognizes more readily.

It is often said of Churchill that he was a better leader in times of war than during peacetime, and that his second tenure as Prime Minister turned out to be an anti-climax. Partly due to failing health and partly due to rapidly changing times, Churchill struggled to galvanize the public in the way he had during the war years.

COMFORT BREAK

Although at one time allies during the wartime coalition, Winston Churchill and Clement Attlee put any previous sense of comradery firmly to one side when facing each other across the floor of the House of Commons. In fact, there is an unsubstantiated story that during one particularly long and drawn out debate in Parliament, both Churchill and Attlee were praying for the division bell to ring – as both were desperate for a comfort break.

When the bell finally rang, both men leapt to their feet and hurried for the gents in the lobby. Being fleeter on his feet than Churchill, Attlee reached the urinal first – when Churchill entered, Attlee noticed him start and shyly take a step back. 'A bit stand-offish today, aren't we Winston?' said Attlee coyly. To which Churchill is alleged to have replied, 'No, it's just that whenever you see something huge Clement you try and nationalize it'.

Highly decorated
Other medals, honours and accolades

Churchill once said that history would be kind to him because he intended 'to write it'. In the event, he didn't need to champion his own part in World War II – after 1945 many countries and institutions rushed to bestow honours, accolades and tributes upon him. Streets and squares in

Churchill in 1946

the UK and across the globe were renamed after Churchill, and new public buildings such as libraries, theatres and hospitals took his name, as did schools and colleges. It must have been exhausting work trying to keep up with the number of ceremonies and services invoked in his honour. Below is a list of some of the more significant or unusual decorations and titles that Churchill received both before and after World War II.

Knight Companion of the Most Noble Order of the Garter (1953)

When Queen Elizabeth II knighted Churchill in 1953, the decision was taken to also make him a Knight Companion of the Order of the Garter. An exclusive honour, this can only be granted by the reigning monarch, in contrast to other honours that are usually determined by the incumbent Prime Minister. King Edward III instigated the Order of the Garter in the 14th century, and membership of the order has since remained limited to the monarch,

the Prince of Wales, and no more than 24 Knight Companions. The honour is traditionally bestowed for gallantry and chivalry befitting of a knight, and is ranked as the third highest honour in the UK behind the Victoria Cross and the George Cross. Candidates for the Order of the Garter are always announced on St George's Day, 23 April.

Order of Merit (1946)

Soon after the end of the war, King George VI invited Churchill to join the Order of Merit. Membership of this order is not restricted to citizens of the UK, but can also include citizens from Commonwealth countries. There can only be 24 living members of the order at any one time, and the honour isn't restricted to distinguished military service personnel, but may also include notable people from science, business, politics and the arts. Current members of the order include the playwright Tom Stoppard, and the artist, David Hockney.

Order of the Companions of Honour (1922)

Churchill joined the Order of the Companions for his services to politics in the 1920s. This order is open to Commonwealth countries and is sometimes considered to be a lesser version of the Order of Merit. It consists of a maximum of 65 living members and is awarded for distinguished achievement and service to the arts, politics, religion and culture. Current members include the theatre director

Companions of Honour badge

Peter Brook, and the naturalist and broadcaster, Sir David Attenborough.

In addition to receiving high honours and membership of exclusive orders, Churchill was also decorated for his military career, and many different countries also paid him tributes. Below is a list of these medals and citations; the year the medals were authorized is in brackets after each entry, as this sometimes differs from the military campaigns or periods of service to which they relate.

British medals

India Medal, 1895, Punjab Frontier 1897–98, UK (1898)

Queen's Sudan Medal, 1896–98, UK (1899)

Victory Medal, UK (1920)

Africa Star, UK (1945)

British War Medal, 1914–18, UK (1919)

France and Germany Star, UK (1945)

Italy Star, UK (1945)

1939–45 Star, UK (1945)

1914–15 Star, UK (1919)

Queen's South Africa Medal,
1899–1902, Diamond Hill,
Johannesburg, Relief of
Ladysmith, Orange Free State,
Tugela Heights, Cape Colony,
UK (1901)
Defence Medal, 1939–45, UK (1945)
War Medal, 1939–45, UK (1946)
King George V Coronation Medal,
UK (1911)
King George V Silver Jubilee Medal,
UK (1935)
King George VI Coronation Medal,
UK (1937)
Queen Elizabeth II Coronation
Medal, UK (1953)
Territorial Decoration, King
George V, UK (1924)

Non-British medals

Cross of the Order of Military
Merit, Red Ribbon, First Class,
Spain (1896)
Grand Cordon of the Order
of Leopold with Palm,
Belgium (1945)
Knight Grand Cross, Order of the
Lion of the Netherlands,
Holland (1946)
Grand Cross, Order of the Oaken
Crown, Luxembourg (1946)

Grand Cross with Chain, Royal
Norwegian Order of St Olav,
Norway (1948)
Order of the Elephant,
Denmark (1950)
Order of Liberation, France (1958)
Most Refulgent Order of the
Star of Nepal, First Class,
Nepal (1961)
Grand Sash of the High Order
of Sayyid Mohammed bin
Ali el Senoussi, Kingdom of
Libya (1962)
Army Distinguished Service Medal,
USA (1919)
War Cross with Palm,
Belgium (1945)
Military Medal 1940–45,
Luxembourg (1946)
Military Medal, France (1947)
War Cross with Palm,
France (1947)
Cuban Campaign Medal, 1895–98,
Spain (1914)
Khedive's Sudan Medal, Khartoum,
Egypt (1899)
King Christian X's Liberty Medal,
Denmark (1946)
Order of the White Lion,
Czech Republic (posthumously
awarded 2014)

King Christian X's Liberty Medal

Other notable achievements and accolades

Churchill was awarded the Nobel Prize for Literature in 1953, and President John F. Kennedy successfully petitioned Congress to make Churchill an Honorary Citizen of the United States of America in 1963. Moreover, Churchill also enjoyed widespread recognition in the world of academia. Alongside the creation of Churchill College at Cambridge, he received honorary degrees and doctorates from several leading British universities, including the University of Aberdeen, the University of Liverpool, the University of London, and Queens University, Belfast. In addition, Churchill also received honorary doctorates from universities in the USA (including a doctorate in Law from Harvard), Canada, Denmark and the Netherlands, and served as Chancellor of Bristol University and as Rector of Edinburgh University – both largely ceremonial appointments. Finally, after World War II Churchill was granted Freedom of the City status in no fewer than 23 different British cities, as well as a total of 42 cities across the globe – this far exceeds the number ever granted to any other British citizen in history.

MOVABLE CHURCH

In 1946, Churchill gave a memorable speech at Westminster College in Fulton, Missouri, USA, known as the 'Sinews of Peace' or 'Iron Curtain' speech. A couple of decades later in the 1960s, Westminster College was eager to commemorate the 20th anniversary of Churchill's epoch-defining speech, so an ambitious plan was devised to build a lasting memorial to the man.

St Mary the Virgin Aldermanbury

The college raised funds to purchase the remains of a church designed by Sir Christopher Wren in London. The church of St Mary the Virgin Aldermanbury had something of a chequered history, having been first built in the 12th century, only to be destroyed by the Great Fire of London in 1666. The highly acclaimed architect Sir Christopher Wren subsequently rebuilt the church in distinctive Portland stone, but sadly the structure was damaged yet again by German bombers during the Blitz of World War II.

Thus, in the 1960s, Westminster College had the church dismantled piece by piece, and the stones were shipped across the Atlantic and rebuilt within the campus grounds, according to Wren's original designs and drawings. Today, the basement of the church contains a permanent exhibition and interactive displays dedicated to Churchill's life and works, and has been ratified by the US government as America's National Churchill Museum.

Glittering career
Horseracing success with Colonist II

Winston Churchill enjoyed a lifelong love of horses, which stemmed from an early age. He learned his horsemanship skills at his preparatory school in Hove (see Fresh Air) then he served for a time as a cavalryman. Therefore it was perhaps no surprise when in 1949, at the age of 75, Churchill took up racehorse ownership as a hobby.

Churchill's father, Lord Randolph Churchill, had been an enthusiastic horse owner, whose thoroughbred L'Abbesse De Jouarre famously won the 1889 Epsom Oaks. As is tradition in the world of horse racing, Churchill took over his father's racing colours of 'pink with chocolate sleeves' when he registered as an owner with the Jockey Club in 1949. In fact, when Churchill College at Cambridge was established in 1960, it adopted the Churchill racing colours as the colours of the official college scarf.

Churchill had been encouraged to participate in the sport by his son-in-law, Christopher Soames, who persuaded him to purchase a French-bred three-year-old grey thoroughbred colt named Colonist II. Although a 'maiden' (as yet to win a race in three attempts) in France, Soames clearly thought that the horse had the potential to improve. He convinced Churchill that if they could get the horse some 'black type' (win a graded race), its bloodstock value would greatly inflate.

Up to that point, Churchill had experienced something of a chequered history with the racing public. During his controversial tenure as Chancellor of the Exchequer in the mid-1920s, he had introduced a tax on betting that had so enraged on-course bookmakers that they went on strike, refusing to take bets at race meetings. Churchill was subsequently forced to repeal the tax. However, when it was suggested at the height of the Blitz in early 1941 to suspend all race meetings, Churchill persuaded his Cabinet to allow the sport to continue, albeit in a truncated form, arguing that such pastimes were a benefit to public morale.

In any event, Colonist II was sent to the stables of the Epsom trainer Walter Nightingall, who was to remain Churchill's trainer of choice throughout his career as a racehorse owner. Churchill's charge made his British racecourse debut at Salisbury in late summer 1949, making light work of a field of maidens and winning by a cosy 4 lengths. Colonist II quickly followed up with two more

Churchill at the races in 1946

victories, one of which was a wide-margin win in the now prestigious Ribblesdale Stakes – run at Royal Ascot in contemporary times, but previously forming part of Ascot's September race meeting. Colonist II failed to win another race as a three-year-old, probably due to a dislike for soft autumn ground. But the decision was made to keep the horse in training for at least another season.

Colonist II began his four-year-old campaign in April 1950 in the Spring Handicap at Salisbury where he finished a dissapointing fourth. Nightingall the trainer assured Churchill and Soames that the horse had needed the race and would show marked improvement next time. In the meantime, Churchill had his eyes on a race named in his honour at the now defunct racecourse of Hurst Park in Surrey a few weeks later. Soames was unsure that Colonist II would win, advising Churchill not to bet on his horse as it was running in a very competitive race. In the event, Soames was proved right – but Colonist II came a gallant second, displaying the battling qualities that would become the horse's hallmark for the rest of its racing career.

Throughout the summer and autumn of 1950, Colonist II ran on another nine occasions, chalking up a hugely impressive eight victories that included notable wins in stakes races at Kempton, 'Glorious' Goodwood, and Sandown Park – with his only defeat coming in the Ascot Gold Cup at Royal Ascot. Colonist II finished off a glittering four-year-old racing career by winning the Jockey Club Cup at Newmarket in October 1950. Running over an extended trip of 2 miles and 2 furlongs across the stamina-sapping undulations of Newmarket Heath, the racehorse, weary after a long season and giving weight to his rivals, prevailed by a length and a half, much to the jubilation of the crowd. Racing journals highly praised the performance of Colonist II during his four-year-old season, with one publication commenting that the horse had dominated the season and performed 'miracles'.

Colonist II continued to run as a five-year-old, winning two more races, including the Winston Churchill Stakes at Hurst Park, a race that had eluded him the previous season. In doing so he defeated King George VI's horse, Above Board. Churchill wrote to Princess Elizabeth after the race to thank her for her 'gracious congratulations', saying that he wished there was a way for both horses to have been winners.

An injury caused by losing a shoe in a race at Glorious Goodwood in August curtailed Colonist II's racing career, and the horse was sold to a stud farm at the end of season sales. Churchill had initially been strangely reticent about selling his beloved horse to stud, and is believed to have responded to Walter Nightingall's suggestion with the comment: 'To stud? And have it said that the Prime Minister of Great Britain is living off the immoral earnings of a horse?'

Churchill continued to own race horses right up until a year before his death. Backtracking on his previous views, he purchased a small stud farm in Surrey where he bred several notable horses, including Vienna who won several high-profile races in the early 1960s. In 1964 Churchill wrote to Walter Nightingall to thank him for his services, saying that he would be winding up his racing operation as ill-health prevented him from watching his beloved horses run. In the letter, Churchill reserved a special mention for Colonist II, and described how indebted he was to his son-in-law Christopher Soames for persuading him to invest in the horse in the first place.

HAPPY COINCIDENCE

On the 24 January 2015, 50 years to the day since the death of Winston Churchill in 1965, a horse named Winston Churchill contested a five-runner handicap chase at Uttoxeter Racecourse in Staffordshire. Trained by Sophie Leech and ridden by jockey Killian Moore, the horse handsomely rewarded punters who may have noticed the coincidence by romping home to win by an astonishing 81 lengths.

Although a fairly low grade race, Winston Churchill's victory attracted a good deal of media attention. Leech told the press afterwards that the horse's owner, a Mr G. Thompson, was a 'huge fan' of the real Winston Churchill, and that the plan had always been to find a race on the anniversary of the statesman's death to commemorate the day.

End of an era
Death and state funeral

Churchill died quietly in his sleep on 24 January 1965 – by curious coincidence this was the 70th anniversary of the death of his father, Randolph. Churchill had suffered a stroke on 9 January and had remained bedridden at his home in Hyde Park Gate, London, attended by his wife and eldest daughter. The announcement of Churchill's death was made by a BBC news bulletin at 8am – within hours, large crowds of mourners had gathered outside the Churchill home to pay their respects. Owing to his failing health, plans had long been in place for Churchill's funeral.

By decree of Queen Elizabeth II it was decided that Churchill's body should 'lie in state' at Westminster Hall in the Houses of Parliament then be honoured with a full state funeral. This is an honour rarely granted to anyone other than royalty, and Churchill was the first person to be granted one since Prime Minister William Gladstone. This decision proved

to be popular with the general public – thousands of people queued outside Parliament to file past Churchill's coffin, adorned with the Union Jack inscribed with the insignia of the Knights of the Garter, to pay their final respects. In fact, it is estimated that over 320,000 people visited Westminster Hall to bid Churchill farewell over the following three days.

The funeral was scheduled to take place on 30 January 1965, the following Saturday. On that day, thousands of people lined the streets of London to see Churchill's coffin transported by a Royal Navy gun carriage through the centre of the city to St Paul's Cathedral. The funeral party started their journey from Westminster Hall at 9.45am, after a single solitary chime from Big Ben. On arrival at St Paul's Cathedral, six members of the armed forces carried Churchill's coffin up the steps.

Inside the cathedral more than 6,000 people, six sovereigns and 15 heads of state were in attendance. In total, over 120 countries sent envoys or representatives, with Elizabeth

II leading the mourners alongside the Churchill family. Meanwhile the ceremony was broadcast live across the world and watched by around 350 million people, including over 25 million people in the UK alone. The audience for the broadcast in the USA outstripped that for the funeral of President John F. Kennedy, a testament to the ennormous popularity Churchill enjoyed there.

In contrast to the Duke of Wellington and Lord Nelson, two other former recipients of state funerals, Churchill declined the offer to be buried in St Paul's, opting instead for a burial at the family plot at St Martin's Church in Bladon, Oxfordshire. So Churchill's coffin was taken to a jetty close to Tower Hill then carried aboard a service vessel, the MV *Havengore,* for transportation down the Thames. The boat set off on its journey adorned by a 19-gun salute – as it passed by the long stretch of quays along the route, crane drivers bowed their cranes in reverance and respect. The Royal Airforce also staged a fly-by of Lightning fighter aircraft.

Churchill's grave at St Martin's Church, Bladon

Churchill's coffin was then transferred to Waterloo station and placed aboard a specially chartered steam train for the short journey to Oxford. All along the line, people turned out in their hundreds to stand on the platforms as the train passed. Once at Oxford, all the churches rang their bells to herald Churchill's arrival at his final resting place. Lady Clementine, Churchill's wife, is said to have declared to her daughter Mary Soames that the day 'Wasn't a funeral, it was a triumph'.

Lights, camera, action!
Appearing on screen

There is a wealth of newsreel footage available of Winston Churchill. However, according to the Internet Movie Database (IMDB), there have also been 34 feature films and 22 television programmes made that include actors portraying him. It should be noted that the character of Churchill only appears as a cameo role in many of these productions, played by the actor shown in the list below:

Film appearances
Royal Cavalcade (1935) – C.M. Hallard

Captains of the Clouds (1942) – Miles Mander (voice only)

Mission to Moscow (1943) – Dudley Field Malone

Stalingradskaya Bitva I (1949) – Viktor Stanitsyn

Due Mogli Sono Troppe (1950) – Pietro Meloni

Nezabyvaemyy God 1919 (1952) – Viktor Stanitsyn

Above Us the Waves (1955) – Peter Cavanagh (voice only, uncredited)

The Man Who Never Was (1956) – Peter Sellers (voice only, uncredited)

The Siege of Sidney Street (1960) – Jimmy Sangster (uncredited)

The Finest Hours (1964) – Patrick Wymark (adult Churchill, voice only), George Westbury (young Churchill, voice only)

A King's Story (1965) – Patrick Wymark (voice only)

Operation Crossbow (1965) – Patrick Wymark

Liberation (1970) – Yuri Durov

Young Winston (1972) – Simon Ward

The Eagle has Landed (1976) – Leigh Dilley

Picassos äventyr (1978) – Sune Mangs

Sekret Enigmy (1979) – Józef Zacharewicz

Le Bourreau des Coeurs (1983) – René Douglas

Katastrofa w Gibraltarze (1984) – Wlodzimierz Wiszniewski

Jane and the Lost City (1987) – Richard Huggett

Casablanca Express (1989) – John Evans

Caro Dolce Amore (1994) – John Evans

Shaheed Uddham Singh: Alais Ram Mohammad Singh Azad (2000) – Joe Lamb

Operación Gónada (2000) – Craig Stevenson

Two Men Went to War (2002) – David Ryall

The Gathering Storm (2002 film) – Albert Finney, for HBO

The Virgin of Liverpool (2003) – Paul Barber (uncredited)

Churchill: The Hollywood Years (2004) – Christian Slater

Allegiance (2005) – Mel Smith

I Am Bob (2007) – Ian Beyts

Inglourious Basterds (2009) – Rod Taylor

Into the Storm (2009) – Brendan Gleeson, for HBO

The King's Speech (2010) – Timothy Spall

Paradox (2010) – Alan C. Peterson

Television appearances

The Valiant Years (1960–63) – Richard Burton

The Gathering Storm (1974) – Richard Burton

Days of Hope (1975) – Leo Britt (Churchill appears in one episode of Ken Loach's controversial mini-series)

Eleanor and Franklin: The White House Years (1977) – Arthur Gould-Porter

Churchill and the Generals (1979) – Timothy West

Winston Churchill: The Wilderness Years (1981) – Robert Hardy

The Winds of War (1983) – Howard Lang

War and Remembrance (1988) – Robert Hardy

Timothy Spall

Timothy West

Bomber Harris (1989) –
  Robert Hardy
'Allo 'Allo!, Series 7, Episode 4,
  'Up the Crick Without a Piddle'
  (1991) – John James Evanson
  (as John James Evans)
The Lost World (2001) – Linal Haft
Bertie and Elizabeth (2002) –
  David Ryall
The Gathering Storm (2002) –
  Albert Finney

Wallis and Edward (2005) –
  David Calder
The Sittaford Mystery (2006) –
  Robert Hardy
Into the Storm (2009) –
  Brendan Gleeson
Doctor Who 'The Beast Below',
  'Victory of the Daleks',
  'The Pandorica Opens',
  'The Wedding of River Song'
  (2010–11) – Ian McNeice
Horrible Histories (2009–) –
  Jim Howick
Peaky Blinders (2013) –
  Andy Nyman, (2014) –
  Richard McCabe
Murdoch Mysteries, 'Winston's Lost
  Night' – Thomas Howes
Churchill: The Lost Interviews (2014)
  – Richard Beenham
Up the Women, 'Train' (2015) –
  Harry Peacock

SELECTED BIBLIOGRAPHY

Best, Geoffrey, *Churchill: A Study in Greatness*, Penguin (2002)

Bonham-Carter, Violet, *Winston Churchill As I Knew Him*, Collins (1965)

Churchill, Randolph S. and Gilbert, Martin, *Winston S. Churchill*,
   Heinemann (1967–82)

Churchill, Winston, *A History of the English-Speaking Peoples*,
   Cassell (1956–58)

Churchill, Winston, *Lord Randolph Churchill*, Macmillan (1907)

Churchill, Winston, *Marlborough His Life and Times*, Sphere (1967)

Churchill, Winston, *My Early Life: A Roving Commission*, Thornton
   Butterworth (1930)

Churchill, Winston, *The Second World War*, Cassell (1948–54)

Churchill, Winston, *The Story of the Malakand Field Force 1897*, Longman,
   Green & Co. (1899)

Churchill, Winston, *The World Crisis*, Thornton Butterworth (1923–31)

Gilbert, Martin, *Churchill: The Wilderness Years*, Macmillan (1981)

Graebner, Walter, *My Dear Mr Churchill*, Michael Joseph (1965)

Jenkins, Roy, *Churchill: A Biography*, Pan (2002)

Johnson, Boris, *The Churchill Factor: How One Man Made History*,
   Hodder (2015)

Kelly, Brian and Smyer, Ingrid, *The Best Little Stories of Winston Churchill*,
   Cumberland House Publishing (2008)

Langworth, Richard M. (ed.), *Churchill in His Own Words*,
   Ebury Press (2012)

Nel, Elizabeth, *Mr Churchill's Secretary,* Hodder & Stoughton (1958)

Rhodes James, Sir Robert, *Churchill: A Study in Failure, 1900–1939*,
   Weidenfeld & Nicolson (1970)

Singer, Barry, *Churchill Style: The Art of Being Winston Churchill*,
   Abrams Image (2012)

Soames, Mary, *Clementine Churchill*, Cassell (1979)

Taylor, A. J. P., *English History 1914–1945*, Oxford University Press (1965)

Toye, Richard, *Churchill's Empire: The World That Made Him and the World He Made*, Pan (2011)

Toye, Richard, *The Roar of the Lion: The Untold Story of Churchill's World War II Speeches*, Oxford University Press (2013)

ACKNOWLEDGEMENTS

Extracts from the following speeches by Winston Churchill are licensed under the terms of the Open Parliament License v3.0:

'The Locust Years', 12 November 1936
Official Report (*Hansard*) citation:
**HC Deb 12 November 1936
vol 317 cc1081–155**

'The War at Sea', 11 April 1940
Official Report (*Hansard*) citation:
**HC Deb 11 April 1940
vol 359 cc733–64**

'Blood, Toil, Tears And Sweat',
13 May 1940
Official Report (*Hansard*) citation:
**HC Deb 13 May 1940
vol 360 cc1501–25**

'We Shall Fight on the Beaches',
4 June 1940
Official Report (*Hansard*) citation:
**HC Deb 04 June 1940
vol 361 cc787–98**

'Their Finest Hour', 18 June 1940
Official Report (*Hansard*) citation:
**HC Deb 18 June 1940
vol 362 cc51–64**

'The Few', 20 August 1940
Official Report (*Hansard*) citation:
**HC Deb 20 August 1940
vol 364 cc1132–274**

Reproduced with permission of Curtis Brown, London on behalf of the Estate of Winston S. Churchill. Copyright © Winston S. Churchill

INDEX

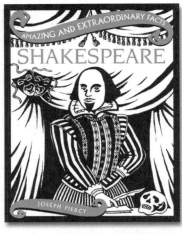

Amazing and Extraordinary
Facts: Shakespeare
Joseph Piercy
ISBN: 978-1-910821-06-0

Amazing and Extraordinary
Facts: London at War
Stephen Halliday
ISBN: 978-1-910821-08-4

Amazing and Extraordinary
Facts: London
Stephen Halliday
ISBN: 978-1-910821-02-2

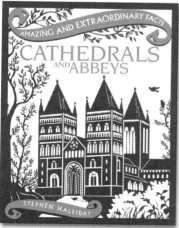

Amazing and Extraordinary
Facts: Cathedrals and Abbeys
Stephen Halliday
ISBN: 978-1-910821-04-6

For more great books visit our website at **www.rydonpublishing.co.uk**

THE AUTHOR

J oseph Piercy is a freelance writer and journalist who is the author of
several books on subjects that range from the history of the English
language, to philosophy and popular culture, including *The Story of English,
Symbols* and *The 25 Rules of Grammar*. Joseph holds a Master of Philosophy
Degree in creative writing and literary stylistics from the University of
Wolverhampton, and he is an Associate Research Fellow at the University
of Sussex. Joseph lives in his hometown of Brighton with his wife and
daughter, and a very old cat.

Joseph Piercy is also the author of *Amazing and Extraordinary
Facts: Shakespeare*.

AUTHOR ACKNOWLEDGEMENTS

I 'd like to offer my heartfelt thanks to the following people and
institutions whose help and support has been invaluable in the
composition of this book: Robert Ertle and Freya Dangerfield, my editor,
for suggesting the project in the first place, and for their patience and
support; James Fleet and R. L. Lucas for their additional material and
research, and all the staff at the University of Sussex Library for their kind
use of the facilities in which to immerse myself in all things Churcillian;
and all my family and friends for putting up with constant comments along
the lines of 'I never knew Churchill did this and that' based trivia.

PICTURE CREDITS